SpringerBriefs in Economics

For other titles published in this series, go to
http://www.springer.com/series/8876

Walter Manshanden · Wouter Jonkhoff
Editors

Infrastructure Productivity Evaluation

Springer

Editors
Walter Manshanden
TNO (Dutch Organization for Applied
Scientific Research)
2600 AA, Delft
The Netherlands
walter.manshanden@tno.nl

Wouter Jonkhoff
TNO (Dutch Organization for Applied
Scientific Research)
2600 AA, Delft
The Netherlands
wouter.jonkhoff@tno.nl

ISBN 978-1-4419-8100-4 e-ISBN 978-1-4419-8101-1
DOI 10.1007/978-1-4419-8101-1
Springer New York Dordrecht Heidelberg London

Springer is part of Springer Science+Business Media (www.springer.com)

Contents

Contributors

Carlijn C. Bijvoet
ING Economic Department, Amsterdam, The Netherlands
carlijn.bijvoet@mail.ing.nl

Martijn I. Droës
TNO, Built Environment and Geosciences, Van Mourik Broekmanweg 6,
2628 XE Delft, The Netherlands
and
Utrecht University, Utrecht School of Economics, Janskerkhof 12,
3512 BL Utrecht, The Netherlands
m.droes@uu.nl

Wouter Jonkhoff
TNO (Dutch Organization for Applied Scientific Research),
2600 AA, Delft, The Netherlands
wouter.jonkhoff@tno.nl

Carl C. Koopmans
SEO Economic Research, Roetersstraat 29, 1018 WB Amsterdam,
The Netherlands
c.koopmans@seo.nl

Bart Kuipers
Erasmus School of Economics, Erasmus University Rotterdam, P.O. Box 1738,
3000 DR Rotterdam, The Netherlands
bkuipers@ese.eur.nl

Jenny E. Ligthart
Department of Economics and Center, Tilburg University, P.O. Box 90153,
5000 LE Tilburg, The Netherlands
j.ligthart@uvt.nl

Walter Manshanden
TNO (Dutch Organization for Applied Scientific Research),
2600 AA, Delft, The Netherlands
walter.manshanden@tno.nl

Rosa M. Martin Suárez
Tilburg University, Tilburg, The Netherlands

Menno Rustenburg
TNO Innovation and Environment, Delft, The Netherlands

Chapter 1
Introduction

Walter Manshanden and Wouter Jonkhoff

Abstract This introductory chapter of the publication illuminates the need for advanced infrastructure evaluation methods in developed economies, identifying fitting examples from EU member states. First, taking an historical (ex post) perspective improves the degree of realism in ex ante evaluations. Second, productivity plays a pivotal role in infrastructure evaluation, enabling the policy maker to appreciate the influence of the existing infrastructure network on benefits of network extensions. The authors proceed by summarising on the written contributions to the volume. In the remainder of the book, evaluation methods are assessed to various policy levels, such as regional investment policy, harmonisation of infrastructure appraisal in the EU setting, harbour policy and cohesion issues.

Keywords Capital • Commuting • Cost–benefit analysis • Ex post evaluation • Industrial policy • Infrastructure • Ports • Productivity • Public choice • Regional policy • Roads • Subsidies

1.1 Infrastructure: What Does the Rear-View Mirror Tell Us About the Way Forward?

At the start of the second decade of the twenty-first century, the European Union is faced with profound challenges. Two main issues are the recent eastward extension of the Union and the need for reform, enhancing efficient management and public support. One of the pivotal subjects in this respect is the European Cohesion Policy (ECP), aiming at diminishing regional economic disparities. Infrastructure plays a central role in ECP investments. New EU members have generally less developed

W. Manshanden (✉)
TNO (Dutch Organization for Applied Scientific Research),
2600 AA, Delft, The Netherlands
e-mail: walter.manshanden@tno.nl

W. Manshanden and W. Jonkhoff (eds.), *Infrastructure Productivity Evaluation*,
SpringerBriefs in Economics 1, DOI 10.1007/978-1-4419-8101-1_1,

networks of roads, railways, stations and airports than the EU-15 do. Considerable network extensions are enabled by cohesion funds, similar to those spent for infrastructure development in Spain, Portugal and Ireland in the 1980s and 1990s. Infrastructure deserves a serious appraisal given its heterogeneous nature and its general economic importance. Hence, infrastructure evaluation is rightly at the centre of academic and policy interest.

Several long-time EU member states have a wealth of experience in infrastructure assessment and planning. These countries include Germany, the UK, France and the Netherlands. Germany features the most extensive and high-quality motorway network in the EU. France's TGV network has been path-breaking in the European long-distance rail network. The Netherlands, despite its small size, harbours Europe's largest port (Rotterdam) and the EU's fifth largest international airport (Schiphol).

To be sure, history matters in this respect. The productivity of new infrastructure depends to a large degree on existing infrastructure. For example, the strategic position of the Netherlands in North-west Europe comes at a price mirrored in decreasing network productivity and rising negative externalities of infrastructure. By the same token, Dutch taxpayers are facing relative large bills to maintain and extend the infrastructure that supports the country's key role in international trade.

Indeed, investments usually incur certain current costs and uncertain future positive and negative benefits. We might refer to the Dutch Golden Age saying that "the cost precedes the benefit". How, then, should infrastructure initiatives be evaluated? Despite recent European integration and other signs of increased mobility resulting from globalisation and the rise of information technology, EU member states have done less than satisfactory to arrive at comparable infrastructure evaluation methods. National guidelines for cost–benefit and multiple criteria analysis exist, but these appear far from homogeneous. At the same time, much is done to improve ECP evaluation. The EU provides European cost–benefit analysis guidelines, but the extent to which these are used remains unclear.

While its importance for policy making is undisputed, evaluating infrastructure prior to construction (ex ante evaluation) suffers from a number of serious drawbacks. The most prominent disadvantage is the political pressure to arrive at positive results of evaluations. This can result in biased evaluation incentives, in which costs of infrastructure projects are usually estimated too low, abstaining from uncertainties in construction, maintenance and external risks. Alternatively, negative externalities are omitted, or positive effects exaggerated.

Ex post analysis offers the opportunity of looking with the benefit of hindsight. Instead of uncertain future benefits, historical data on one single reality instead of multiple future scenarios can be used to arrive at real benefits, provided these data exist and deal with recent use of infrastructure. Usually, policy interest in ex post analysis is less than enthusiastic, as politicians and other decision makers deal with the future rather than with the past. Nevertheless, taking the rear-mirror view might offer interesting insights into the way forward, notably in the European setting. The experience in existing EU member states can be very instructive on optimal investment options in the new member states. Taking a capital productivity view on infrastructure can offer valuable insights on policy issues that are central to governments throughout the developed world, such as the choice between new investment and maintenance of existing motorways, railways or waterways.

For the Dutch Regional Science Association, the interest in ex post analysis has been the reason to organise a meeting in 2004 on ex post evaluation of infrastructure. The conference was chaired by the Netherlands Applied Scientific Research Institute TNO. Respected researchers with extended national and international experience in the academic as well as consultancy environment were invited to present papers based on their ongoing work on ex post analysis. They delivered working papers reflecting both national and international experience. TNO eventually decided to publish the book in English, considering the continuing relevance of infrastructure evaluation in the European policy arena after the major enlargements of the EU in 2004 and 2007, and the generally high quality of the papers presented.

Ligthart and Martin Suarez deal with the contribution of public capital to private output using a meta-analysis and a meta-regression analysis. They point out that reported estimates of the output elasticity of public capital show considerable heterogeneity. Nevertheless, they conclude that the return on public capital is substantially above the marginal return of private capital, suggesting that investment in public capital should be encouraged from a macroeconomic point of view.

Koopmans and Bijvoet offer insight into the causal relationships concerning the effect of public subsidies for regional development in the European setting. On a meta-analysis level, they examine how thorough regional policy studies analyse the degree to which desired socio-economic effects are realised, finding a trade-off between research quality and effectiveness appreciation. They conclude that evaluations in the literature offer scant empirical evidence for underpinning policy choices. However, they note that the literature focuses heavily on policies in lagging regions and does not include other types of regional policy.

Kuipers and Jonkhoff provide an historical overview of post-war harbour investment policy in the port of Rotterdam, comparing an ex ante cost–benefit analysis of future investment with their own ex post analysis of major investment in the same area between the 1960s and 2002. They observe how policy intentions are subject to societal paradigm changes, affecting greatly the degree to which the initial investment is effective in the long run.

Manshanden and Droës calculate the contribution of capital and labour to growth and total factor productivity for regions in the Netherlands, especially focusing on the peripheral north of the country. They find that investment in public capital contributed 17–21% to economic growth in the Netherlands, which is in line with the findings of Ligthart and Martin Suarez in the first chapter. However, this estimate varies by region; it is larger in the periphery of the Netherlands. The results suggest that public capital accumulation contributes to regional economic growth in the Netherlands but that other factors, such as innovation and entrepreneurship, may be more important to achieve long-term economic growth.

Jonkhoff and Rustenburg investigate EU member states' appraisal of indirect effects of transport investment. They argue that due to increasing mobility and decreasing returns to infrastructure networks, integrated appraisal of transport projects is urgently needed. Harmonisation of the different national evaluation methods is needed, further than what has been achieved so far to attain international comparability of transport initiatives.

We hope that the reader will enjoy the variety of research that the authors offer and that policy makers as well as researchers gain some insight and further ideas for their decisions (which are ex ante by nature) and research.

Chapter 2
The Productivity of Public Capital: A Meta-analysis

Jenny E. Ligthart and Rosa M. Martin Suárez

Abstract The paper measures the contribution of public capital to private output using a simple meta-analysis and a meta-regression analysis based on panel data. We find an output elasticity of public capital of 0.14 in the random effects model, which is substantially smaller than the simple arithmetic average value of 0.20. Reported estimates of the output elasticity of public capital show considerable heterogeneity. We identify the type of public capital, the level of aggregation of the public capital data, the country type, the econometric specification, and publication bias as sources of variation.

Keywords Infrastructure • Meta-analysis • Meta-regression analysis • Public capital stock • Public investment

2.1 Introduction

Discussions among academics and policy makers about the contribution of the public capital stock to private output have been ongoing during the last two decades. Recently, this debate has revived within the European Union (EU), primarily driven by two developments. First, the Lisbon Agenda agreed by EU leaders in March 2000 – which aims to create a climate that stimulates economic growth, competitiveness, and innovation in Europe – has put growth issues back on the European policy agenda. The second is the renewed interest in fiscal policy rules since the inception of the Stability and Growth Pact, which applies to countries forming the

J.E. Ligthart (✉)
Department of Economics and Center, Tilburg University, P.O. Box 90153, 5000 LE Tilburg, The Netherlands
e-mail: j.ligthart@uvt.nl

W. Manshanden and W. Jonkhoff (eds.), *Infrastructure Productivity Evaluation*, SpringerBriefs in Economics 1, DOI 10.1007/978-1-4419-8101-1_2,

Economic and Monetary Union. Many economists feared that the EU fiscal rules – imposing ceilings of 3 and 60% on the fiscal deficit-to-GDP and public debt-to-GDP ratios, respectively – would have a negative impact on public capital formation. Indeed, in many instances, governments find it easier to cut back on infrastructure investment rather than current expenditure, reflecting the long lags with which reductions in capital expenditures are felt. To provide input to the public capital debate, it is of importance to measure the contribution of public capital to private output.

Various authors have tried to measure the output elasticity of public capital by estimating a production function that includes the public capital stock as an input. Aschauer (1989, 1990) was one of the first to investigate this issue for the USA in an attempt to explain the productivity growth slowdown in the 1970s.[1] Indeed, public investment fell, and aggregate labour productivity growth declined slightly later, providing casual evidence of a linkage. Aschauer (1989) found in his econometric study that a 1% rise in the public capital stock increased private output by 0.39%. Since then, many studies have been undertaken for the USA and various other OECD countries. The findings of these studies generally extend from a significantly negative effect to a strongly positive effect of public capital on output.[2] So far, researchers have not attached much priority to reconciling these differences.

We quantitatively review the literature on the effects of public capital on private output by means of meta-analysis. In addition, we employ meta-regression analysis to analyze the determinants of observed heterogeneity across and between studies. Drawing on Stanley and Jarrell (1989) and Stanley (2001), meta-analysis can be defined as a body of statistical methods to summarize, evaluate, and analyze empirical results from primary studies. A problem with conventional reviews of the literature is that empirical studies are difficult to compare, owing to differences in theoretical specifications, employed empirical methodologies, and data definitions. Meta-analysis presents a more systematic and objective way to summarize empirical results. In addition, it allows us to explain the wide study-to-study variation by fundamental economic variables and the researcher's choice of research design. In this way, an estimate of the output elasticity of public capital can be derived, which researchers and policy makers can use as an input into their analyses.[3]

[1] Mera (1973) was the first study that estimated for nine Japanese regions a production function including some form of public capital, which he refers to as "social capital." For example, transportation and communications facilities, soil and water conservation, health and educational facilities. The work of Mera was followed by two papers by Ratner (1983) and Da Costa et al. (1987).

[2] Only a small number of studies have been reported. More details on the output elasticities of public capital can be found in Table 2.1 below.

[3] Meta-analysis has a long-standing tradition in psychological and medical research. Environmental and transport economists were the first to apply meta-analysis in economics in the 1980s. Since then, it has been picked up by researchers in other fields in economics such as labour economics (e.g., Card and Krueger 1995), industrial organization (e.g., Button and Weyman-Jones 1992), and international economics (e.g., De Mooij and Ederveen 2003).

Although various authors have reviewed the literature on the productivity of public capital,[4] only one study (i.e., Button 1998) has applied a meta-regression analysis. Button's (1998) analysis covers 26 studies, which are published during 1973–1994. His analysis yields a bare minimum of 28 data points. Our paper extends Button's study in four ways. First, our sample for the meta-analysis covers all relevant studies up to and including the year 2005, giving rise to a meta-dataset of 49 studies. Our larger meta-regression dataset – also including studies not reporting any standard errors – incorporates 55 studies and encompasses 248 observations. Second, we conduct a standard meta-analysis in addition to a meta-regression analysis to arrive at a *meta* output elasticity of public capital. Third, we test for a larger set of potential determinants of differences across studies, including variables describing the functional and econometric specification of the production function, the capital stock definition, and the level of economic development. Finally, Button (1998) employs a pooled ordinary least squares (OLS) model in its meta-regression analysis,[5] whereas we exploit the panel structure of the data by taking multiple observations from the same study. We estimate various standard panel data models, namely, the fixed effects model, the random effects model, and an extended Generalized Least Squares (GLS) model, which corrects for heteroscedasticity in the error term. In view of the larger number of observations and use of more advanced estimation techniques, we expect to find more efficient and reliable estimates.

Our analysis finds an output elasticity of public capital of 0.14 in the random effects meta-analysis model, which is substantially below the simple average of 0.20 and the value of 0.39 initially found by Aschauer (1989). Reported estimates show a substantial amount of observed heterogeneity. Studies employing core infrastructure, using data at the national level, featuring publication bias, and estimating the equation in logarithmic levels find larger output elasticities of public capital. In contrast, studies using data for the USA and imposing an economies-of-scale restriction on the coefficients of the production function find smaller output elasticities of output.

The remainder of the chapter is structured as follows. Section 2.2 discusses definitions, presents the various methodological approaches used to estimate the impact of public capital on private output, and studies stylized facts. In addition, it gives an overview of the criticisms launched against the main approach, that is, the production function approach. Section 2.3 describes the meta-sample and presents the results of a simple meta-analysis. Section 2.4 formulates hypotheses to explain differences across studies and presents results of the meta-regression analysis. Section 2.5 concludes the chapter.

[4]See the studies by Munnell (1991, 1992), Gramlich (1994), Pfahler et al. (1996), Button (1998), Sturm et al. (1998), Button and Rietveld (2000), Mikelbank and Jackson (2000), IMF (2004), and Romp and De Haan (2007).

[5]Button's (1998) analysis is basically a cross-sectional approach given the limited number of observations.

2.2 Public Capital and Private Output

What do we mean by infrastructure investment? How is this related to the public capital stock? Which concept of public capital is typically used in empirical analyses? These questions need to be addressed before we venture into the methodology of measuring the output effects of public capital.

2.2.1 *Definitions*

Gramlich (1994, p. 1177) defines infrastructure capital from an economic point of view as "large capital intensive natural monopolies such as highways, other transportation facilities, water and sewer lines, and communications systems." Although most of these systems are publicly owned, in some cases, they are privately owned, for example, a firm that constructs its own road to connect itself to the main highway. The literature generally defines infrastructure capital based on ownership.

Most studies employ a *narrow definition* of public capital that includes the tangible capital stock owned by the public sector, excluding military structures and equipment. More specifically, the intangible capital stock covers *core infrastructure*, hospitals, educational buildings, and other public buildings. Core infrastructure in turn consists of roads, railways, airports, and utilities such as sewerage and water facilities (Aschauer 1990). Some studies use a *broad definition* of public capital by including human capital investment (e.g., Garcia-Milà and McGuire 1992) or health and welfare facilities (e.g., Mera 1973). The latter components are hard to measure, which explains why most authors focus on narrowly defined public capital.

The concept of public capital may also differ owing to differences in the level of government at which it is measured. Various studies focus on the national public capital stock, including all levels of governments (federal, state, and local), for example, Aschauer (1989), whereas others deal only with capital stocks defined at the regional level (e.g., Garcia-Milà and McGuire 1992) or city level (e.g., Duffy-Deno and Eberts 1991). The majority of studies have a fairly comprehensive coverage including all levels of government.

2.2.2 *Methodologies Employed in the Literature*

The services of public capital are almost never sold on markets, except for toll fees for highway use, which makes it difficult to assess the economic value of public capital. Nevertheless, economists have estimated the stock of public capital, which is subsequently used as an input into the production function approach (see below). To measure the public capital stock, the perpetual inventory method is employed, which is based on an estimate of the initial value of the capital stock to which gross investment flows are added and from which technical depreciation of the existing stock – based on the expected lifespans of the various types of assets – is subtracted.

2.2.2.1 Four Methodological Approaches

The literature has distinguished four approaches that study empirically the link between private output and public capital: the production function, vector autoregression (VAR), behavioural, and growth regressions approach. The production function approach is the most widely known and applied.[6] This approach considers the stock of public capital either as a separate input in private production (which we call the pure production function approach) or as a factor improving multifactor productivity (which is known as the growth accounting approach, as explored by Hulten and Schwab 1991b). In both cases, public capital is assumed to be strictly exogenous.

The VAR approach analyzes the relationships between public capital, private inputs, and private output without imposing a theoretical structure a priori. The multi-equation VAR approach – generally employing the same set of variables as in the production function approach – models every endogenous variable as a function of its own lagged value and the lagged values of the other endogenous variables and can therefore assess whether there is any feedback effect from private sector variables to the public capital stock.

The remaining two approaches yield elasticities that are incomparable with the output elasticities of public capital derived by both the production function and VAR approach. First, the behavioural approach, coined as such by Sturm et al. (1998), which employs cost or profit functions to assess whether public capital reduces firms' production costs or increases firms' profits. Second, the cross-country growth regressions approach, which specifies a reduced-form equation to estimate – using cross-sectional or panel data – the relationship between per capita private output growth and the public investment-to-GDP ratio. The growth regressions approach should be distinguished from studies that embed a production function in an estimated Ramsey type growth model. We classify the latter under the pure production function approach if an output elasticity of public capital is derived.

2.2.2.2 The Production Function Approach

Because the majority of studies in our database concern the production function approach, we discuss this approach in more detail. The cornerstone of the production function approach is a production function that incorporates the stock of public capital G_t as an input:

$$Y_t = A_t F\left[K_t, G_t, L_t\right], \tag{2.1}$$

[6]The surveys of Sturm et al. (1998) and Romp and De Haan (2007) identify 54 studies employing some form of production function approach. In 2005, the other three approaches feature the following number of papers: 21 studies concern VAR studies; 26 studies deal with cost or profit functions; and 12 studies use growth regressions.

where Y_t is real aggregate private output of a jurisdiction (region or country), A_t is an index of economy-wide productivity, K_t denotes the stock of (non-residential) private fixed capital, and L_t denotes employment (generally measured by total hours worked), $F[.]$ describes a general functional form, and t denotes time. The general idea of the production function approach is that the services of public capital are proportional to the stock of public capital – which is generally assumed to be a pure public good – and in that way enhance private output. Equation (2.1) shows that public capital may affect aggregate private output in two ways. The first is a direct effect, that is, $\partial F_t / \partial G_t > 0$. Second, public capital may raise private production by increasing the economy-wide productivity index, that is, $A_t(G_t)$, with $\partial A_t / \partial G_t > 0$. Equation (2.1) assumes Hicks-neutral public capital, which is a common assumption made in the public capital literature.[7]

Most studies employ a Cobb–Douglas production function:

$$Y_t = A_t K_t^{\alpha} G_t^{\beta} L_t^{\gamma}, \qquad \alpha, \beta, \gamma > 0 \tag{2.2}$$

where $\beta \equiv dlnY_t / dlnG_t$ is the output elasticity of public capital, which is hypothesized to be positive. This specification imposes a unit elasticity of substitution between factors of production. Furthermore, public capital and private inputs are cooperative factors of production, implying that a rise in G_t increases the marginal productivity of labour and private capital.

Taking natural logarithms on both sides of (2.2) we get a linearized specification:

$$lnY_t = lnA_t + \alpha lnK_t + \beta lnG_t + \gamma lnL_t \tag{2.3}$$

Equation (2.3) can readily be estimated in logarithmic levels or first differences of logarithmic levels (i.e., growth rates) to arrive at estimates of $\alpha, \beta,$ and γ. As can be seen from (2.3), the productivity index enters the equation in an additive way. Accordingly, it does not make a difference whether public capital enters the production function directly (as a separate input) or indirectly through the technology index. Following Aschauer (1989), many studies include a constant and a time trend as a proxy for technological progress (i.e., $lnA_t = a_0 + a_1 t$, where $a_0 > 0$ and $a_1 > 0$).

Incorporating public capital into the production function raises the issue of returns to scale in production. Imposing the restriction of constant returns to scale across all inputs in (2.1), which is represented by $\alpha + \beta + \gamma = 1$, yields

$$ln(Y_t / K_t) = lnA_t + \beta\, ln(G_t / K_t) + \gamma\, ln(L_t / K_t), \tag{2.4}$$

which features decreasing returns with respect to private inputs taken together (i.e., $\alpha + \gamma < 1$). Instead of using private capital productivity $ln(Y_t/K_t)$ as the left-hand side variable, some studies subtract lnL_t from both sides of (2.3) so as to arrive at

[7] Hicks-neutral public capital enters the production in such a way that the average and marginal products of all factors increase in the same proportion.

labour productivity as the dependent variable. An alternative model assumes constant returns to scale in private inputs (represented by $\alpha + \gamma = 1$):

$$ln(Y_t / K_t) = lnA_t + \beta lnG_t + \gamma ln(L_t / K_t), \tag{2.5}$$

allowing for increasing returns to scale across all inputs (i.e., $\alpha + \beta + \gamma > 1$).

Alternatively, various authors[8] have employed a translog specification, which nests many commonly used functional forms (including the Cobb–Douglas production function):

$$\begin{aligned} lnY_t = {} & lnA_t + \alpha lnK_t + \beta lnG_t + \gamma lnL_t \\ & + a_k (\ln K_t)^2 + a_G (lnG_t)^2 + a_L (lnL_t)^2 \\ & + b_{LK} lnL_t lnK_t + b_{LG} lnL_t lnG_t + b_{KG} lnK_t lnG_t, \end{aligned} \tag{2.6}$$

where a_i for $i = \{K, L, G\}$ and b_{jk} for $j = \{K, L\}$ and $k = \{G, K\}$ are parameters. The translog specification allows for non-unitary and non-constant elasticities of substitution between inputs. A potential problem in its use is that the second-order terms may give rise to multicollinearity. Consequently, many authors have resorted to the more restrictive Cobb–Douglas form.

2.2.3 Stylized Facts

The output elasticity of public capital can be rewritten to yield the marginal productivity of public capital, that is, $\partial Y_t / \partial G_t = \beta (Y_t / G_t)$, which is an indicator of the effective rate of return on government capital.[9] To assess whether investments in public capital are worthwhile, policy makers generally compare the marginal productivity of public capital with the marginal productivity of private capital, which equals the real rate of interest in a competitive market.

Gramlich (1994) argues that the return on public capital derived by Aschauer (1989) is too large to be credible. Indeed, depending on the year, it varies between 60 and 80%. The marginal output gain of an additional unit of private capital estimated from Aschauer's equation amounts to 30%, suggesting a difference between public and private capital of a factor two to three. Some observers (e.g., Aschauer 1990) point to the high rate of return found in R&D studies to justify the high output elasticities found in the early literature. Others (including Gramlich), however, argue that a large share of public capital is directed at less productive sectors of the economy such as waste treatment and pollution abatement, which is unlikely to contribute much to national output.

[8]Early adopters of the translog specification are, amongst others, Merriman (1990), Pinnoi (1994), and Dalamagas (1995).

[9]Here, it is assumed that public capital is remunerated based on its marginal productivity. Aaron (1990) has argued that in the presence of government pricing inefficiencies and the absence of markets, this is not a very realistic assumption.

Munnell (1992) is less pessimistic about the usefulness of empirical studies on public capital. First, studies published in the mid-1990s find lower – and thus more realistic – values of the output elasticity of public capital. Second, most studies find a positive and statistically significant output elasticity of public capital. What do the narrative surveys tell us about the evidence? The range of β estimates is wide, varying from negative values to values that are well in excess of that of private capital. The majority of studies, however, find a significantly positive elasticity (Stylized Fact 1). Ligthart (2002) derives an unweighted average of the output elasticity of public capital of 0.25 for OECD countries (if the production function is estimated in logarithmic levels), which is substantially below Aschauer's estimate.

Stylized Fact 1 *Public capital has a significant and positive effect on private output.*

The first author studying the output effect of public capital in a regional context is Mera (1973), who analyzes nine Japanese regions, employing a broad definition of public capital. Since then, various authors have found elasticities at the regional level that are much smaller than those from analyses using aggregate data for a single country (Stylized Fact 2), reflecting spillover effects.[10] Intuitively, some of the beneficial effects of public capital accrue to neighbouring regions and therefore cannot be internalized at the level of an individual region. In a Nash equilibrium – when governments set their optimal level of public goods provision given the level set by other governments – both regions end up with a less than socially optimal stock of public capital. Spillovers can be formalized as follows:

$$Y_{it} = A_{it} K_{it}^{\alpha} G_{it}^{\beta} G_{jt}^{\eta} L_{it}^{\gamma}, \tag{2.7}$$

where G_{it} is the public capital stock of the home region i, G_{jt} is the public capital of the neighbouring region j, and $\eta > 0$ is the spillover effect.[11] The studies by Holtz-Eakin and Schwartz (1995a, b) and Boarnet (1998) find little evidence of spillover effects.

Stylized Fact 2 *The output elasticity of public capital for national-level studies is higher than that of regional-level studies.*

Aschauer (1990), and Sturm and De Haan (1995) stress that the composition of public investment matters for its effect on private production. The stock of core infrastructure (such as roads, railways, and airports) is more productive than other components of public capital such as educational and office buildings and hospitals (Stylized Fact 3). Accordingly, empirical studies that broaden the stock of public capital while staying within the boundaries of the narrow definition – thus necessarily

[10] Munnell (1990), Eisner (1991), Garcia-Milà and McGuire (1992), and Evans and Karras (1994), and Holtz-Eakin (1994).

[11] Some authors argue that spillover effects are likely to be positively related to the population size and the openness of regions, which is not reflected in the above equation.

including less productive components – find a lower β than studies focusing on core infrastructure only.

Stylized Fact 3 *Core infrastructure is more productive than other categories of narrowly defined public capital.*

Button (1998) suggests that the output elasticities derived from production function equations based on first differences of variables are lower than that of studies estimating the equation in levels of variables. However, the dummy variable representing studies based on a first differences specification is not significant in Button's analysis. In contrast, in an overview of studies for OECD countries, Ligthart (2002) reports elasticities derived from production functions estimated in first differences that are significantly higher for equations estimated in levels. No consensus has emerged yet.

2.2.4 Criticisms of the Production Function Approach

The early literature on the output elasticity of public capital has generated a substantial amount of criticism in the 1990s. Various authors have criticized Aschauer's model for being misspecified due to the omission of relevant macroeconomic variables. Tatom (1991) argues that Aschauer's approach is flawed because it omits energy prices, which should be included to account for the decline in the use of private capital induced by higher oil prices during the 1970s. Tatom (1991) and Crowder and Himarios (1997), for example, include energy prices in the production function to capture these kinds of supply shocks. Gramlich (1994), in turn, criticizes Tatom's approach for mixing production functions and cost functions. Instead of including energy prices, studies should employ a measure of the quantity of energy use in production. The study by Vijverberg et al. (1997), for instance, includes imported raw materials in the production function.

Another specification issue concerns the role of capacity utilization in the production function. Generally, production function studies incorporate a capital utilization rate – or, alternatively, the unemployment rate – to capture the effect of business cycle fluctuations on production factor use.[12] Because capacity utilization enters the productive function in an additive fashion in the logarithmic model, it does not affect the optimal capital–labour ratio. Indeed, capacity utilization affects all factor inputs across the board, which is a restrictive assumption. The majority of studies, therefore, do not include capacity utilization in the econometric specification.

Some of the early studies have been criticized for not properly accounting for common trends. Generally, time series on private output and the public capital stock contain a unit root or, in other words, they are non-stationary time series. If variables

[12] For example, Aschauer (1989), Hulten and Schwab (1991a), and Sturm and De Haan (1995) were early adopters of this specification.

are non-stationary, the usual test statistics have non-standard distributions, implying that the application of standard inference procedures gives rise to misleading results. In particular, one may find spurious relationships between inputs and outputs. Some studies have, therefore, proposed to eliminate the trend in variables by taking first differences of the time series.[13] Two criticisms were raised against first differencing. First, the growth rate of private output in a particular year is not strongly correlated with the growth rate in the capital stock during that same year, as lagged effects are likely to be important. Indeed, it may take a number of years before large construction projects are completed and become productive. Second, and related to the previous argument, first differencing may discard information on a possible long-run equilibrium relationship between a set of non-stationary time series, that is, the variables are cointegrated. Consequently, the focus of the analysis is shifted away from the long-run effects of public capital to the short-run effects. Instead of first differencing, the variables should be first tested for cointegration. If variables are cointegrated, it is justified to estimate the equation in levels of variables. In the mid-1990s, various authors have employed the Engle–Granger (1987) test and/or Johansen cointegration (1988) test (generally recognized to be superior to the former), giving rise to mixed results.

Aschauer (1989) and related studies assume that G_t is strictly exogenous, implying that the causality runs from public capital to private output. Some authors (e.g., Munnell 1992; Gramlich 1994) have pointed to the lack of attention paid to feedback effects. The direction of causality may run from output to public capital rather than the other way around. Indeed, higher output may increase the demand for public capital and generate favourable budgetary conditions to support an increase in public investment. Recently, a number of authors[14] have employed VAR models with a view to capture the dynamic interactions between output, public capital, and private capital.

Econometric studies employ very different concepts of public capital, which makes it hard to compare the results of these analyses. Some authors employ narrowly defined public capital [e.g., Canning and Bennathan (2000) study paved roads], whereas others define capital in a broad sense [e.g., Mera (1973) and Mas et al. (1996) employ social public capital]. In addition, the definition of what constitutes public capital (and core infrastructure) may differ by country.

2.3 A Simple Meta-analysis

Meta-analysis can be defined as a body of statistical methods to summarize, evaluate, and analyze results of empirical studies. In doing so, meta-analysis produces value added above and beyond conventional literature reviews, which have less of a quantitative orientation. A meta-analysis forces a researcher to be explicit

[13] See, for example, Aaron (1990), Hulten and Schwab (1991a), and Tatom (1991).

[14] Clarida (1993), Otto and Voss (1996), Batina (1998), Flores de Frutos et al. (1998), Pereira and Roca Sagales (1999), Ligthart (2002), and Pereira and Roca Sagales (2003) have employed a VAR approach amongst others.

about the weights assigned to the studies, whereas conventional literature reviews leave much more room for subjective elements in the analysis. We show that we cannot simply take an average over all studies to derive an estimate of the output elasticity of public capital. Section 2.3.2 conducts a simple meta-analysis based on the meta-sample of Sect. 2.3.1.

2.3.1 The Meta-sample

To estimate the output elasticity of public capital, we focus on studies employing the pure production function and VAR approaches. All the selected production function studies use a log-linearized production function. Consequently, they estimate a uniformly defined output elasticity of public capital, which measures the percentage change in real private output in response to a 1% increase in the public capital stock. We identified via an extensive literature search 60 studies that could potentially be included in our sample. In order to conduct a standard meta-analysis, it is necessary to collect not only the point estimates of the output elasticity but also the precision of the estimates (i.e., their standard errors). Not all studies report standard errors, particularly those employing the VAR approach,[15] which forced us to dismiss 11 studies.[16] We also excluded studies (e.g., Mera 1973) that include non-standard components in their definition of public capital. Our dataset consists of 248 measurements taken from 49 studies, of which 41 are published in academic or professional journals and eight are unpublished.[17]

Table 2.1 presents an overview of the studies included in the meta-sample. We take all relevant elasticities from each study rather than using a single estimate per study.[18] The number of elasticities per study differs, averaging to five, potentially giving rise to dependency between observations from the same study in our meta-sample.[19] Following Aschauer's work, the majority of studies deal with the USA (26 out of 49) at the national or regional level. Only 15 studies pertain to other OECD countries. The remaining eight studies cover multiple countries.

Figure 2.1 shows that there is substantial variation across output elasticities of public capital. On the order of 80% of the estimates takes on values between –0.15

[15]Many VAR studies were not considered for our potential database because they neither reported standard errors nor disclosed any output elasticities.

[16]Studies reporting output elasticities of public capital but not their standard errors are the following: Clarida (1993), Pinnoi (1994), Crihfield and Panggabean (1995), Wylie (1996), Lau and Sin (1997), Mamatzakis (1999), Pereira and Flores de Frutos (1999), Pereira and Roca Sagales (2001), Ashipala and Haimbodi (2003), Pereira and Roca Sagales (2003), and Everaert and Heylen (2004). These studies, however, have been included in the meta-regression analysis of Sect. 2.4.

[17]We could not get a hold of some of the early unpublished papers, thereby making the sample of unpublished papers less representative.

[18]This is still a controversial issue in the literature. Bijmolt and Pieters (2001) claim that all available measurements need to be included, whereas Stanley (1998) believes that only one measurement per study should be selected.

[19]No routines are available yet to measure and correct for this problem.

Table 2.1 Summary statistics of the studies in the meta-dataset

	Authors	Jurisdiction	Output elasticities				
			Number	Mean	Median	Minimum	Maximum
1	Ratner (1983)	USA	2	0.057	0.057	0.056	0.058
2	Aschauer (1989)	USA	1	0.400	0.400	0.400	0.400
3	Ram and Rasmey (1989)	USA	1	0.240	0.240	0.240	0.240
4	Merriman (1990)	US (48 states) and Japan (9 regregions)	4	0.418	0.445	0.200	0.580
5	Munnell (1990)	USA	2	0.360	0.360	0.330	0.390
6	Eisner (1991)	USA (national and 4 regions)	17	0.027	0.064	–0.491	0.383
7	Ford and Poret (1991)	10 OECD countries	20	0.378	0.395	–0.340	0.770
8	Tatom (1991)	USA	2	0.087	0.087	0.042	0.132
9	Berndt and Hansson (1992)	Sweden	1	0.687	0.687	0.687	0.687
10	Garcia-Milà and McGuire (1992)	USA (48 states)	2	0.105	0.105	0.045	0.165
11	Bajo-Rubio and Sosvilla-Rivero (1993)	Spain	1	0.190	0.190	0.190	0.190
12	Finn (1993)	USA	2	0.010	0.010	–0.138	0.158
13	Munnell (1993)	USA (national and 4 regions)	9	0.155	0.120	–0.004	0.380
14	Eisner (1994)	USA	1	0.270	0.270	0.270	0.270
15	Evans and Karras (1994)	7 OECD countries	7	–0.005	0.033	–0.175	0.182
16	Holtz-Eakin (1994)	USA (48 states and 8 regions)	13	0.009	–0.050	–0.130	0.348
17	Ai and Cassou (1995)	USA	4	0.308	0.308	0.295	0.321
18	Baltagi and Pinnoi (1995)	USA (48 states)	16	0.073	0.070	–0.110	0.390
19	Dalamagas (1995)	Greece	1	0.532	0.532	0.532	0.532
20	Holtz-Eakin and Schwartz (1995a)	USA (48 states)	6	0.010	–0.069	–0.022	0.054

21	Holtz-Eakin and Schwartz (1995b)	USA (48 states)	2	0.004	0.004	–0.038	0.046
22	Sturm and De Haan (1995)	The Netherlands and USA	8	0.635	0.540	0.260	1.150
23	Garcia-Milà et al. (1996)	USA (48 states)	18	0.023	–0.011	–0.071	0.370
24	Hulten (1996)	USA	1	0.317	0.317	0.317	0.317
25	Mas et al. (1996)	Spain (17 regions)	4	0.050	0.067	–0.021	0.086
26	Otto and Voss (1996)	Australia	2	0.232	0.232	0.168	0.296
27	Crowder and Himarios (1997)	USA	6	0.291	0.294	0.168	0.382
28	Kavanagh (1997)	Ireland	1	0.495	0.495	0.495	0.495
29	Vijverberg et al. (1997)	USA	1	0.119	0.119	0.119	0.119
30	Batina (1998)	USA	1	–0.110	–0.110	–0.110	–0.110
31	Boarnet (1998)	USA (State of California)	4	0.083	0.056	–0.016	0.236
32	Flores de Frutos et al. (1998)	Spain	1	0.210	0.210	0.210	0.210
33	Ramirez (1998)	Mexico	2	0.315	0.315	0.040	0.590
34	Delorme et al. (1999)	USA	1	0.276	0.276	0.276	0.276
35	Canning and Bennathan (2000)	97 countries	2	0.084	0.084	0.083	0.085
36	Charlot and Schmitt (2000)	France (22 regions)	6	0.229	0.253	0.070	0.321
37	Nourzad (2000)	24 countries	5	0.469	0.445	0.397	0.553
38	Vanhoudt et al. (2000)	15 EU countries	4	0.042	0.050	–0.093	0.161
39	Yamano and Ohkawara (2000)	Japan (47 regions)	1	0.034	0.034	0.034	0.034
40	Yamarik (2000)	USA (48 states)	4	0.087	0.081	0.025	0.160
41	Stephan (2001)	France (21 regions) and Germany (11 states)	6	0.100	0.099	0.083	0.128
42	Yilmaz et al. (2001)	USA	1	0.032	0.032	0.032	0.032
43	Kemmerling and Stephan (2002)	87 German cities	3	0.169	0.169	0.169	0.170

(continued)

Table 2.1 (continued)

	Authors	Jurisdiction	Output elasticities				
			Number	Mean	Median	Minimum	Maximum
44	Ligthart (2002)	Portugal	18	0.189	0.194	0.022	0.371
45	Dodonov et al. (2002)	13 Eastern European countries	2	0.525	0.525	0.450	0.600
46	Song (2002)	Australia	1	0.005	0.005	0.005	0.005
47	Stephan (2003)	Germany (11 states)	3	0.659	0.651	0.547	0.779
48	Kamps (2005)	22 OECD countries	23	0.452	0.551	–0.568	1.265
49	La Ferrara and Marcellino (2005)	Italy (4 regions)	5	0.017	–0.139	–0.148	0.367
			248	0.200	0.136	–0.568	1.265

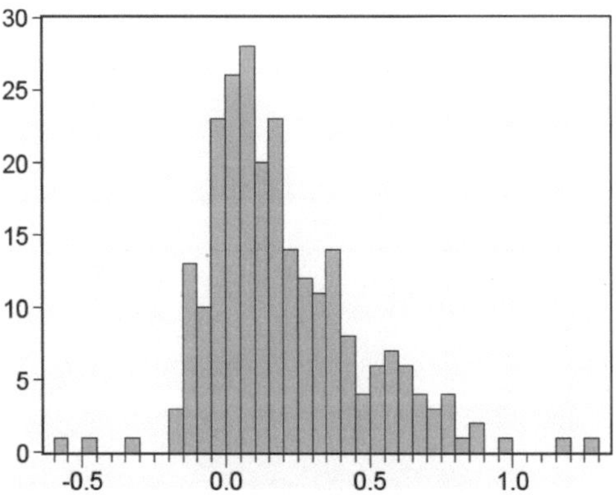

Fig. 2.1 Distribution of the output elasticity of public capital. Notes: The horizontal axis measures the output elasticity of public capital and the vertical axis the frequency

and 0.40. The multi-country study of Kamps (2005) reports both the largest elasticity (1.26 for Denmark) and the smallest elasticity (–0.57 for Portugal). Roughly 21% (52 out of 248) of the output elasticity estimates have a negative sign, of which 75% (39 out of 52) is statistically significant at the 5% level. The small percentage of significantly negative output elasticities in our sample provides a quantitative underpinning of Stylized Fact 1.

The simple (or arithmetic) average of the output elasticity of public capital in our meta-sample is 0.20, whereas the median elasticity amounts to 0.13, reflecting a distribution that is skewed to the right. Of course, the mean of the distribution is just a naive estimate that does not take into account the difference in precision with which the output elasticities are estimated. The sample consists of 13 outliers (5% of total) that are two standard deviations (i.e., two times 0.265) above or below the mean. If these extreme values were deleted, the simple mean would fall to 0.175, a decline of only 12.5%, which is sufficiently small to leave the outliers in.

2.3.2 Results of the Meta-analysis

If estimates of the effect size (i.e., β) are considered to be homogeneous – and thus differences between estimates are due to purely random variation – a fixed effects model is the appropriate specification. However, often there are systematic differences between effect size estimates, in which case they are considered to be heterogeneous. In case of heterogeneity of effect size estimates, a random effects model should be selected.[20] The random effects specification assumes that there is unobserved heterogeneity across observations.

[20]The causes of heterogeneity can be assessed by means of a meta-regression analysis. See Sect. 2.2.4.

Table 2.2 Meta-analysis for various study characteristics and specifications

Study category	Sample size	Mean 1/	Confidence interval Lower bound	Upper bound
(a) Fixed effects				
All studies	248	0.039	0.037	0.040
Aggregation level				
National-level study	137	0.014	0.012	0.016
Regional-level study	111	0.049	0.046	0.052
Econometric specification				
Variables in logarithmic levels	136	0.023	0.022	0.025
First differences of logarithms	112	0.037	0.030	0.043
(b) Random effects				
All studies	248	0.139	0.125	0.154
Aggregation level				
National-level study	137	0.200	0.177	0.224
Regional-level study	111	0.092	0.075	0.109
Econometric specification				
Variables in logarithmic levels	136	0.133	0.118	0.147
First differences of logarithms	112	0.169	0.135	0.203

1/ Weighted mean

Table 2.2 shows the results of the meta-analysis for both the fixed effects and random effects meta-analysis model.[21] To determine which model to use, we have applied Cochran's (1954) Q test:

$$Q \equiv \sum_{i=1}^{n} \omega_i T_i^2 - \frac{\left(\sum_{i=1}^{n} \omega_i T_i\right)^2}{\sum_{i=1}^{n} \omega_i}, \tag{2.8}$$

where T_i is the estimate of the "true" effect in study i (i.e., our β), ω_i is the weight of study i, and n is the total number of β estimates. In the fixed effects model, ω_i is the inverse of the variance of the ith estimate (or "within study" variation). In the random effects model, ω_i is the inverse of the sum of the "within" and "between" study variance. The Q value amounts to 10,017. Comparing this value with the critical value of a $\chi^2(248)$ distribution leads us to conclude that we can reject the null hypothesis of no heterogeneity. Consequently, differences between point estimates of studies are not purely random but are the result of observed heterogeneity across studies. This result is not surprising given that the studies differ considerably in the type of public capital considered, the countries covered, and the functional and econometric specifications employed.

[21] See Hedges (1994) for an exposition of how this terminology differs from that used in the panel data literature.

The random effects estimate of the output elasticity of public capital of the full sample is 0.14, which falls within the calculated 95% confidence interval [panel (b) of Table 2.2]. As we can see from panel (a) of Table 2.2, the fixed effect estimator is quite small (β is 0.04), but it is an incorrect estimator in view of the results of the Q test. Note that both the fixed and random effects estimators are much smaller than the arithmetic average, reflecting the effect of the weighting scheme. Panel (b) of Table 2.2 shows that the weighted average estimate of the output elasticity for national-level studies is 0.20, which is substantially larger than that of regional-level studies, and thus supports Stylized Fact 2. In addition, the output elasticity for studies estimating variables in levels is 0.13, which falls short of the elasticity estimate of a model employing first differences.

2.4 Meta-regression Analysis

Our goal is to analyze the effects of fundamental variables (such as country characteristics and definitions of public capital) and of different functional and econometric specifications on the output elasticity of public capital. In the meta-regression, we try to verify the stylized facts of Sect. 2.3.2 and various hypotheses that are set out in Sect. 2.4.1. After presenting the hypotheses and meta-regression model, we discuss the econometric results.

2.4.1 Hypotheses

Hulten and Schwab (1991a), Button (1998), and Button and Rietveld (2000) have pointed to the potential differential impact that public investment may have on output depending on the size of the capital stock that has already been installed. In view of the law of diminishing returns in factor accumulation, economies that have already accumulated a large stock of public capital experience a smaller output elasticity. Given that data on capital stocks are not readily available, we proxy a country's capital stock by the level of per capita Gross domestic product (GDP). Therefore, we hypothesize to find a lower β in more developed countries (as measured by a high per capita GDP).

Hypothesis 1 *The output elasticity of public capital depends negatively on the level of development of an economy as measured by its per capita GDP.*

In view of the above, we expect countries other than the USA – which has been the main focus of the public capital literature – to have a larger output elasticity than that of the USA (Corollary 1).

Corollary 1 *Studies for the USA produce a lower* β *than studies for other countries.*

Estimates of the output elasticity are likely to be sensitive to the specification of the production function. As argued in Sect. 2.3.2, various authors have imposed restrictions on the coefficients of the production function to force, for example, constant returns to scale with respect to all inputs [(2.4)] or constant returns to scale in private inputs [(2.5)]. We expect these restrictions to reduce the absolute size of the estimated output elasticity of public capital (Hypothesis 2).

Hypothesis 2 *Studies imposing a constant-returns-to-scale restriction on the parameters of the production function yield a smaller* β *than studies not imposing any restrictions.*

Estimates of the output elasticity of public capital are likely to be sensitive to the econometric specification of the equation to be estimated. In view of the results of Ligthart (2002) and those from the meta-analysis in Sect. 3.2, we hypothesize to find a larger β for studies estimating equations in first differences [Hypothesis 3(a)]. In addition, the size of the output elasticity is also affected by the type of dataset employed, that is, panel or cross-sectional data vs. time-series data [Hypothesis 3(b)]. Because cross-sectional studies are generally conducted at the regional level, we expect both study characteristics to be positively correlated.[22] Hence, in view of Stylized Fact 2, we anticipate to find a smaller β in cross-sectional studies than in single-country time-series studies.

Hypothesis 3 *A smaller* β *results for studies: (a) estimating variables in logarithmic levels rather than in first differences of logarithms, and (b) employing panel data or cross-sectional data.*

Some authors of meta-regression analyses (e.g., De Mooij and Ederveen 2003) have tried to identify the presence of publication bias, which is the tendency to publish only significant results supporting the hypothesis put forward.[23] In our case, we expect to find a larger β in published studies than in unpublished manuscripts [Hypothesis 4(a)]. Because we experienced difficulties in getting a hold of all unpublished papers that we are aware of – possibly biasing the publication dummy variable – we also include an indicator of the significance of the estimated β [Hypothesis 4(b)]. Furthermore, unpublished manuscripts may be published in the near future, which is particularly relevant for recently issued manuscripts containing high-quality research. Alternatively, we include the number of observations to measure publication bias. Intuitively, studies based on a larger sample yield more efficient estimates – and thus more often yield significant parameter estimates – and are therefore less likely to be subject to publication bias [Hypothesis 4(c)].

Hypothesis 4 *(a) Published studies are expected to report a larger* β*; (b) The significance of* β *and its size are positively related; and (c) Studies containing a large number of observations are less likely to suffer from publication bias and thus report a smaller* β.

[22] In the meta-regression analysis, we include both types of study characteristics.

[23] Note that authors may not report unsatisfactory results, which, of course, cannot be measured by a meta-analysis.

2.4.2 Meta-regression Model

2.4.2.1 Methodology

We employ an unbalanced panel consisting of N studies each of which covers J_i estimates of the output elasticity β. The panel is unbalanced because the number of estimates differs by study. The model to be estimated is as follows:

$$Y_{ij} = \pi + \sum_{k=1}^{K} \theta_k X_{ij}^k + \sum_{l=1}^{L} \varphi_l D_{ij}^l + \varepsilon_{ij}, \qquad i = 1,\ldots,N, \qquad j = 1,\ldots,J_i, \tag{2.9}$$

where Y_{ij} is the jth output elasticity of public capital reported in study i, π is an intercept, X_{ij} is a set of K continuous variables (X^1 is per capita GDP of the country for which elasticity estimate j of study i was obtained and X^2 is the number of observations of that study), D_{ij}^l is a set of L dummy variables, and ε_{ij} is an i.i.d. error term. The parameters θ_k and φ_l measure the impact on the output elasticity of study characteristics k and l, respectively.

The following L dummy variables are included (1) D^1 is 1 for core infrastructure and 0 for all other types of public capital (including the total public capital stock), (2) D^2 is 1 for studies pertaining to the USA and 0 otherwise, (3) D^3 is 1 for national-level studies and 0 otherwise, (4) D^4 is 1 if the variables in the study are estimated in levels and 0 otherwise, (5) D^5 is 1 if a returns-to-scale restriction on the coefficients of the production function is imposed and 0 otherwise, (6) D^6 is 1 if panel data are used and 0 otherwise, (7) D^7 is 1 if cross-sectional data are used and 0 otherwise, (8) D^8 is 1 if the coefficient is significant (at the 1 or 5% level) and 0 otherwise, and (9) D^9 if the study is published and 0 otherwise. Based on the stylized facts and hypotheses, the expected signs are as follows: $\theta_1 < 0$, $\theta_2 < 0$, $\varphi_1 > 0$, $\varphi_2 < 0$, $\varphi_3 > 0$, $\varphi_4 < 0$, $\varphi_5 < 0$, $\varphi_6 < 0$, $\varphi_7 < 0$, $\varphi_8 > 0$, and $\varphi_9 > 0$.

2.4.2.2 Data

Our meta-regression sample consists of 282 observations. We took the 49 studies from our meta-analysis sample (see Sect. 2.3.1), from which we dropped five cross-country studies[24] because these could not be matched to a particular country. We have added back in the 11 studies not reporting any standard errors – which are not used in the meta-regression analysis – to obtain 55 studies.[25] In the panel data models, we have grouped the observations by study. The average group size

[24]The cross-country studies are as follows: Evans and Karras (1994), Canning and Bennathan (2000), Nourzad (2000), Vanhoudt et al. (2000), and Dodonov et al. (2002).

[25]Of course, we could have also used the standard errors in weighting the observations. To maximize the number of observations, we decided against this. Any references to "fixed effects" and "random effects" pertain to the standard panel data methods rather than the terminology as employed by meta-analysts.

amounts to 5.1 observations with a maximum number of 2 observations. Alternatively, if we had grouped the observations by country – which allows for an analysis of country-fixed effects – the number of groups would have become relatively small (i.e., only 13 countries).

2.5 Results

Table 2.3 summarizes the empirical findings. We have employed various estimation methodologies: (1) pooled OLS, (2) panel fixed effects, (3) panel random effects, and (4) feasible GLS. The pooled OLS results in column 1 – which forces a common slope and intercept – show that only a few of the explanatory variables are significant. The intercept is significant taking on a value closely in line with the unweighted average found in the meta-analysis. Only the dummies for the USA, panel studies and significance are statistically significant, which is roughly in line with the analysis of Button (1998), who finds only a significant and negative US dummy. Studies on the USA tend to find, ceteris paribus, lower output elasticities than studies conducted for other countries or geographical areas (Corollary 1), reflecting the large stock of infrastructure installed in the USA. We cannot find, however, evidence of a negative relationship between the per capita GDP and the size of the output elasticity.

By pooling reported estimates we cannot analyze unobservable study-specific fixed effects that are likely to be relevant. Therefore, a panel fixed effects model is estimated as shown in column 2 of Table 2.3. The F test for the significance of the fixed effects cannot reject the null hypothesis of insignificant study-specific fixed effects.[26] The panel fixed effects model performs poorly. Only the significance dummy is statistically significant. The results for the panel random effects model – presented in column 3 – are not much better, which is not surprising given the presence of heteroscedasticity in the residuals.[27] Consequently, the fixed effects and random effects models are inappropriate. In the extended GLS model (see columns 4 and 5), the standard errors are reduced, making a larger number of variables statistically significant.

Table 2.4 reports the correlation coefficients between the dependent and the various explanatory variables. We can see that there is a strong negative correlation (about −0.73) between the panel dummy and the dummy for national-level studies,

[26] The F test amounts to $F(54,217) = 1.91$, which exceeds the critical value.

[27] We could not find any evidence of autocorrelation in the residuals. We have performed a likelihood ratio (LR) test to check for the presence of cross-panel heteroscedasticity. The LR test is based on the difference between the unrestricted model, which allows for heteroscedasticity, and the restricted model, which assumes a constant variance of the residuals. The LR test in Table 2.3 shows that the unrestricted model performs better, implying that the error structure is heteroscedastic.

Table 2.3 Results of the meta-regression analysis 1/ 2/

Explanatory variables		Pooled OLS	Fixed effects	Random effects	Feasible GLS	
					Model A	Model B
		(1)	(2)	(3)	(4)	(5)
Constant		0.184***	–	0.149	0.169***	0.043
		(0.073)		(0.095)	(0.049)	(0.044)
GDP per capita	X^1	0.152	0.082	0.090	0.034	–0.004
		(0.190)	(0.276)	(0.212)	(0.114)	(0.123)
Number of observations	X^2	–0.00004	–0.00010	–0.00004	–0.00003***	–0.00004***
		(0.00002)	(0.00017)	(0.0003)	(0.00001)	(0.00001)
Dummy core infrastructure	D^1	0.041	–0.009	0.023	0.050**	0.068***
		(0.040)	(0.063)	(0.046)	(0.022)	(0.022)
Dummy USA	D^2	–0.210***	–0.139	–0.188***	–0.170***	–0.142***
		(0.038)	(0.104)	(0.049)	(0.019)	(0.024)
Dummy national	D^3	0.006	–0.069	–0.002	–0.010	0.065***
		(0.051)	(0.094)	(0.060)	(0.020)	(0.022)
Dummy levels	D^4	–0.021	0.084	0.017	0.005	0.053***
		(0.038)	(0.061)	(0.043)	(0.013)	(0.015)
Dummy restriction	D^5	–0.075	–0.046	–0.042	–0.062***	–
		(0.040)	(0.069)	(0.047)	(0.017)	
Dummy panel	D^6	–0.136***	0.475	–0.136	–0.161***	–
		(0.052)	(0.296)	(0.071)	(0.027)	
Dummy cross section	D^7	–0.079	0.146	0.016	–0.091	–0.032
		(0.092)	(0.113)	(0.099)	(0.074)	(0.068)
Dummy significance	D^8	0.212***	0.192***	0.196***	0.191***	0.143***
		(0.050)	(0.055)	(0.049)	(0.017)	(0.024)
Dummy published	D^9	0.041	–	0.063	0.029	0.002
		(0.045)		(0.067)	(0.033)	(0.036)

(continued)

Table 2.3 (continued)

	Pooled OLS	Fixed effects	Random effects	Feasible GLS	
				Model A	Model B
Explanatory variables	(1)	(2)	(3)	(4)	(5)
Number of observations	282	282	282	282	282
Adjusted R^2	0.229	0.005	0.242	–	–
F-test	8.57	2.01	–	–	–
Probability > F	0.0000	0.0334	–	–	–
Wald Chi^2 test	–	–	45.2	–	–
Probability > Chi^2	–	–	0.0000	–	–
Log likelihood	–	–	–	89.27	86.75
Likelihood ratio test	–	–	–	193.74	197.66
Probability > Chi^2	–	–	–	0.0000	0.0000

1/ Standard errors are in parentheses
2/ *** and ** indicate statistical significance at the 1 and 5% level, respectively

Table 2.4 Correlation matrix

	Output elasticity	GDP per capita	Number of observations	Core infrastructure	Cross	Levels	National	Panel	Published	Restriction	Significance	US
Output elasticity	1.00											
GDP per capita	0.07	1.00										
Number of observations	–0.22	0.26	1.00									
Core infrastructure dummy	0.23	0.11	–0.15	1.00								
Cross-sectional dummy	–0.06	–0.06	–0.09	–0.03	1.00							
Levels dummy	–0.10	0.04	0.16	–0.03	0.13	1.00						
National dummy	0.22	–0.11	–0.39	0.22	–0.02	–0.45	1.00					
Panel dummy	–0.24	0.14	0.50	–0.25	–0.18	0.29	–0.73	1.00				
Published dummy	–0.17	–0.12	–0.06	–0.38	0.11	0.26	–0.11	0.12	1.00			
Restriction dummy	0.11	–0.03	–0.20	0.11	–0.08	–0.27	0.48	–0.39	0.09	1.00		
Significance dummy	0.16	0.08	0.08	–0.06	–0.05	0.05	–0.01	0.21	0.14	0.19	1.00	
US dummy	–0.38	–0.17	0.09	–0.38	0.15	0.09	–0.12	0.10	0.53	–0.11	0.04	1.00

reflecting that most regional studies employ panel data. In addition, the strong positive correlation between the returns-to-scale restriction dummy and the dummy for national-level studies indicates that restrictions are more prevalent in national-level studies. To take into account this collinearity, we have estimated two models (labeled A and B), where model B leaves out the restriction and panel dummies.

Columns 4 and 5 of Table 2.3 present the extended GLS results for models A and B. Besides the significance of the US dummy, five additional explanatory variables are significant in model A. Core infrastructure is shown to be more productive than other types of infrastructure (Stylized Fact 3). Restrictions on the coefficients of the production function reduce the output elasticity of public capital, which is in line with Hypothesis 2. In addition, studies employing panel data yield a smaller output elasticity of public capital. Accordingly, Hypothesis 3(b) is supported, but no collaborating evidence for Hypothesis 3(a) can be found. Studies with a significant β give rise to a larger output elasticity of public capital, which supports Hypothesis 4(b). Finally, we also see that studies with a larger number of observations give rise to a smaller value of β, also suggesting that publication bias may be present. Note that the dummy for national-level studies is insignificant.

Model B shows that the dummies for logarithmic-level and national-level studies are significantly positive if the restriction and panel dummies are dropped from the benchmark equation (model A), supporting the results found in the simple meta-analysis. Compared to model A, it can be seen that the absolute size of the dummy for the USA drops somewhat, whereas the regression intercept falls substantially to a negligible small level and becomes insignificant. The dummy for published studies is insignificant in both models.

2.6 Conclusions

We have used meta-analytical tools to estimate the output elasticity of public capital. The sample features a substantial degree of (observed) heterogeneity. In view of this, we employ a meta-regression analysis to explain the differences between output elasticities of public capital within and between empirical studies.

Our analysis finds an output elasticity of public capital of 0.14 in the random effects model, which is substantially below the simple average of 0.20 and the value of 0.39 initially found by Aschauer. These results suggest a marginal productivity of public capital of 27.5% (assuming a public capital-to-GDP ratio of 51%, like in the USA in the early 2000s). This return is substantially above the marginal productivity of private capital – which is typically reflected in the long-term real rate of interest – suggesting that investment in public capital should be encouraged from a macroeconomic point of view. These results should be interpreted with care given that the simple meta-analysis is just a partial analysis that does not control for other relevant factors. The analysis has not been controlled for observed study heterogeneity yet. The composition of public capital among other factors plays an important role;

more of the same type of public capital does not necessarily boost public capital productivity. In addition, the financing method of public investment spending is not taken into account. Therefore, a careful cost–benefit analysis should precede any additional expenditures on public capital.

The meta-regression analysis – which controls for observed heterogeneity across estimates of the output elasticity of public capital – shows that studies employing core infrastructure, using public capital data at the national level, featuring publication bias, and estimating the equation in logarithmic levels find larger output elasticities of public capital. Studies pertaining to the USA and imposing an economies-of-scale restriction on the coefficients of the production function find smaller output elasticities of public capital.

Our study can be extended in three directions. First, additional explanatory variables could be included in the meta-regression analysis, such as a country's per capita stock of public capital, type of modeling approach (VAR vs. single equation), and type of estimation method. Second, instead of grouping the variables by study in the panel, they could be grouped by country, which allows us to run a meta-regression analysis with country-specific fixed effects. Finally, all observations can be weighted by (a transformation of) the degrees of freedom of the primary study.

References

Aaron HJ (1990) Discussion. In: Munnell AH (ed) Is there a shortfall in public capital investment? Federal Reserve Bank of Boston, Boston

Ai C, Cassou SP (1995) A normative analysis of public capital. Appl Econ 27:1201–1209

Aschauer DA (1989) Is public expenditure productive? J Monet Econ 23:177–200

Aschauer DA (1990) Why is public capital important? In: Munnell AH (ed) Is there a shortfall in public capital investment? Federal Reserve Bank of Boston, Boston

Ashipala J, Haimbodi N (2003) The impact of public investment on economic growth in Namibia. Working paper No. 88. NEPRU, Namibia

Bajo-Rubio O, Sosvilla-Rivero S (1993) Does public capital affect private sector performance? An analysis of the Spanish case. Econ Model 10:179–184

Baltagi BD, Pinnoi N (1995) Public capital stock and state productivity growth: Further evidence from an error components model. Empir Econ 20:351–359

Batina RG (1998) On the long-run effects of public capital and disaggregated public capital on aggregate output. Int Tax Public Finan 94:263–281

Berndt ER, Hansson B (1992) Measuring the contribution of public infrastructure capital in Sweden. Scand J Econ 94:S151–S161

Bijmolt THA, Pieters RGM (2001) Meta-analysis in marketing when studies contain multiple measurements. Mark Lett 12:157–169

Boarnet MG (1998) Spillovers and the locational effects of public infrastructure. J Reg Sci 38:381–400

Button K (1998) Infrastructure investment, endogenous growth, and economic convergence. Ann Reg Sci 32:145–162

Button KJ, Rietveld P (2000) A meta-analysis of the impact of infrastructure policy on regional development. In: Kohno H, Nijkamp P, Poot J (eds) Regional cohesion and competition in the age of globalization. Edward Elgar, Boston

Button K, Weyman-Jones T (1992) Ownership structure, institutional organization, and measured inefficiency. Am Econ Rev 82:439–445

Canning D, Bennathan E (2000) The social rate of return on infrastructure investments. Working paper No. 2390. World Bank, Washington, DC
Card D, Krueger AB (1995) Time-series minimum-wage studies: a meta-analysis. Am Econ Rev 85:238–243
Charlot S, Schmitt B (2000) Public infrastructure and economic growth in France's regions, Working paper, UMR INRA ENESAD, Dijon, France
Clarida RH (1993) International capital mobility, public investment and economic growth. NBER working paper No. 4506. National Bureau of Economic Research, Cambridge, MA
Cochran WG (1954) Some methods for strengthening the common χ^2 tests. Biometrics 10:417–451
Crihfield JB, Panggabean M (1995) Is public infrastructure productive? A metropolitan perspective using new capital stock estimates. Reg Sci Urban Econ 25:607–630
Crowder WJ, Himarios D (1997) Balanced growth and public capital: an empirical analysis. Appl Econ 29:1045–1053
Da Costa SJ, Ellson RW, Martin RC (1987) Public capital, regional output, and developments: some empirical evidence. J Reg Sci 27:419–437
Dalamagas B (1995) A reconsideration of the public sector's contribution to growth. Empir Econ 20:385–414
De Mooij RA, Ederveen S (2003) Taxation and foreign direct investment: a synthesis. Int Tax Public Finan 10:673–693
Delorme CD, Thompson HG, Warren RS (1999) Public infrastructure and private productivity: a stochastic frontier approach. J Macroecon 2:563–576
Dodonov B, von Hirschhausen C, Opitz P, Sugolov P (2002) Efficient infrastructure supply for economic development in transition countries: the case of Ukraine. Post-Communist Econ 14:149–167
Duffy-Deno KT, Eberts RW (1991) Public infrastructure and regional economic development: a simultaneous equations approach. J Urban Econ 30:329–343
Eisner R (1991) Infrastructure and regional economic performance: comment. New Engl Econ Rev September/October:47–58
Eisner R (1994) Real government saving and the future. J Econ Behav Organ 23:111–126
Engle RF, Granger CWJ (1987) Cointegration and error correction: representation, estimation, and testing. Econometrica 55:251–276
Evans P, Karras G (1994) Are government activities productive? Evidence from a panel of US states. Rev Econ Stat 76:1–11
Everaert G, Heylen F (2004) Public capital and long-term labor market performance. J Policy Model 26:95–112
Finn M (1993) Is all government capital productive? Fed Reserve Bank Richmond Econ Q 79:53–80
Flores de Frutos R, Diez MG, Amaral TP (1998) Public capital stock and economic growth: an analysis of the Spanish economy. Appl Econ 322:985–994
Ford R, Poret P (1991) Infrastructure and private sector productivity. OECD working paper 17. OECD, Paris
Garcia-Milà T, McGuire TJ (1992) The contribution of publicly provided inputs to states' economies. Reg Sci Urban Econ 22:229–241
Garcia-Milà T, McGuire TJ, Porter RH (1996) The effects of public capital in state level production functions reconsidered. Rev Econ Stat 78:177–180
Gramlich EM (1994) Infrastructure investment: a review essay. J Econ Liter 32:1176–1196
Hedges LV (1994) Fixed effects models. In: Cooper H, Hedges LV (eds) The handbook of research synthesis. Russel Sage Foundation, New York
Holtz-Eakin D (1994) Public-sector capital and the productivity puzzle, Rev Econ Stat 76:12–21
Holtz-Eakin D, Schwartz AE (1995a) Infrastructure in a structural model of economic growth. Reg Sci Urban Econ 25:131–151
Holtz-Eakin D, Schwartz AE (1995b) Spatial productivity spillovers from public infrastructure: evidence from state highways. Int Tax Public Finan 2:459–468

Hulten CR (1996) Infrastructure capital and economic growth: how well you use it may be more important than how much you have. Working paper No. 5847. NBER, Cambridge, MA

Hulten CR, Schwab RM (1991a) Is there too little public capital: infrastructure and economic growth. Conference paper. American Enterprise Institute, Washington, DC

Hulten CR, Schwab RM (1991b) Public capital formation and the growth of the regional manufacturing industries. Natl Tax J 40:121–134

IMF (2004) Public investment and fiscal policy. Staff memorandum No. SM/04/93. International Monetary Fund, Washington, DC

Johansen S (1988) Statistical analysis of cointegration vectors. J Econ Dyn Control 12:231–254

Kamps C (2005) The dynamic effects of public capital: VAR evidence for 22 OECD countries. Int Tax Public Finan 12:533–558

Kavanagh C (1997) Public capital and private sector productivity in Ireland. J Econ Stud 24:72–94

Kemmerling A, Stephan A (2002) The contribution of local infrastructure to private productivity and its political economy: evidence from a panel of large German cities. Public Choice 113:403–422

La Ferrara E, Marcellino M (2005) TFP, costs, and public infrastructure: an equivocal relationship. In: Artis A, Banerjee A, Marcellino M (eds) The central and eastern European countries and the European Union. Cambridge University Press, Cambridge

Lau P, Sin C-Y (1997) Public infrastructure and economic growth: time-series properties and evidence. Econ Rec 73:125–135

Ligthart JE (2002) Public capital and output growth in Portugal: an empirical analysis. Eur Rev Econ Finan 1:3–30

Mamatzakis EC (1999) Testing for long-run relationship between infrastructure and private capital productivity: a time series analysis for the Greek industry. Appl Econ Lett 6: 243–246

Mas M, Maudos J, Pérez F, Uriel E (1996) Infrastructure and productivity in the Spanish regions. Reg Stud 30:641–650

Mera K (1973) Regional production functions and social overhead: an analysis of the Japanese case. Reg Sci Urban Econ 3:157–186

Merriman D (1990) Public capital and regional output: another look at some Japanese and American data. Reg Sci Urban Econ 20:437–458

Mikelbank BA, Jackson RW (2000) The role of space in public capital research. Int Reg Sci Rev 23:235–258

Munnell AH (1990) Why has productivity growth declined? Productivity and public investment. N Engl Econ Rev January/February:2–22

Munnell AH (1991) Is there a shortfall in public capital investment? An overview. N Engl Econ Rev May/June:2–35

Munnell AH (1992) Policy watch: infrastructure investment and economic growth. J Econ Perspect 6:189–198

Munnell AH (1993) An assessment of trends in and economic impacts of infrastructure investment. In: OECD (ed) Infrastructure policies for the 1990s. OECD, Paris

Nourzad F (2000) The productivity effect of government capital in developing and industrialized countries. Appl Econ 32:1181–1187

Otto GD, Voss GM (1996) Public capital and private production in Australia. South Econ J 62:723–738

Pereira AM, Flores de Frutos R (1999) Public capital accumulation and private sector performance. J Urban Econ 46:300–322

Pereira AM, Roca Sagales O (1999) Public capital formation and regional development in Spain. Rev Dev Econ 3:281–294

Pereira AM, Roca Sagales O (2001) Infrastructure and private sector performance in Spain. J Policy Model 23:371–384

Pereira AM, Roca Sagales O (2003) On the regional impact of public capital formation in Spain. Working paper No. 03.05. Universidad Autonoma de Barcelona, Barcelona

Pfahler W, Hofmann U, Bonte W (1996) Does extra public infrastructure capital matter? Finanzarchiv 53:68–112
Pinnoi N (1994) Public infrastructure and private production: measuring relative contributions. J Econ Behav Organ 23:127–148
Ram R, Rasmey DD (1989) Government capital and private output in the United States: additional evidence. Econ Lett 30:223–226
Ramirez MD (1998) Does public investment enhance productivity growth in Mexico? A cointegration analysis. East Econ J 24:63–82
Ratner JB (1983) Government capital and the production function for US private output. Econ Lett 13:213–217
Romp W, De Haan J (2007) Public capital and economic growth: a critical survey. Perspektiven der Wirtschaftspolitik 8:6–52
Song LL (2002) Public capital, congestion, and private production in Australia, mimeo. University of Melbourne, Melbourne
Stanley TD (1998) New wine in old bottles: a meta-analysis of Ricardian equivalence. South Econ J 64:713–727
Stanley TD (2001) Wheat from chaff: meta-analysis as quantitative literature review. J Econ Perspect 15:131–150
Stanley TD, Jarrell SB (1989) Meta-regression analysis: a quantitative method of literature reviews. J Econ Surv 3:161–170
Stephan A (2001) Regional infrastructure policy and its impact on productivity: a comparison of Germany and France. DIW working paper No. 6748. DIW, Berlin
Stephan A (2003) Assessing the contribution of public capital to private production: evidence from the German manufacturing sector. Int Rev Appl Econ 17:399–418
Sturm J-E, De Haan J (1995) Is public expenditure really productive: new evidence for the USA and the Netherlands. Econ Model 12:60–72
Sturm J-E, Kuper GH, De Haan J (1998) Modelling government investment and economic growth on a macro level: a review. In: Brakman S, van Ees H, Kuipers S (eds) Market behaviour and macroeconomic modelling. MacMillan Press Ltd, London
Tatom JA (1991) Public capital and private sector performance. Fed Reserve Bank St Louis Rev 73:3–15
Vanhoudt P, Matha T, Smid B (2000) How productive are capital investments in Europe? Eur Invest Bank Pap 5:81–106
Vijverberg WPM, Vijverberg C-P, Gamble JL (1997) Public capital and private productivity. Rev Econ Stat 79:267–278
Wylie PG (1996) Infrastructure and Canadian economic growth, 1946–1991. Can J Econ 29:S350–S355
Yamano N, Ohkawara T (2000) The regional allocation of public investment: efficiency or equity? J Reg Sci 40:205–229
Yamarik S (2000) The effect of public infrastructure on private production during 1977–96, mimeo. University of Akron, Akron, OH
Yilmaz S, Haynes K, Dinc M (2001) The impact of telecommunications infrastructure investment on regional and sectoral growth. Aust J Reg Stud 7:383–397

Chapter 3
The Effectiveness of Regional Policy: A Literature Study

Carl C. Koopmans and Carlijn C. Bijvoet

Abstract A survey of the literature shows that research in the effects of regional policy in many cases uses overly simple approaches and highly limiting assumptions. Only a small number of studies measure the effects of policy explicitly and in a scientifically adequate manner. This also goes for the effects of EU cohesion policy: the evidence is thin. Frequently, 50–75% of subsidized jobs and investment turn out to be non-additional. Evaluations in the literature offer only scant empirical evidence for underpinning policy choices.

Keywords Policy effectiveness • Regional development • Regional policy • Regional subsidies

3.1 Introduction

Regional policy has been an integral part of economic policy in developed countries over the last few decades. Many countries have implemented policies to improve the economic performance of lagging regions. The EU has used Cohesion Policy to promote convergence between regions. These policies have different shapes, ranging from employment subsidies (and loans) for firms, to co-financing investments in specific infrastructure, to knowledge transfer and reduction of administrative burdens.

In 2004, the Dutch government has evaluated regional policy by means of a cooperative investigation by several policy departments. Within the framework of the research, we performed a literature study of the effectiveness of regional

C.C. Koopmans (✉)
SEO Economic Research, Roetersstraat 29, 1018 WB Amsterdam, The Netherlands
e-mail: c.koopmans@seo.nl

W. Manshanden and W. Jonkhoff (eds.), *Infrastructure Productivity Evaluation*, SpringerBriefs in Economics 1, DOI 10.1007/978-1-4419-8101-1_3,

policy (Bijvoet and Koopmans 2004). The following questions were central to the study:

- Effectiveness: To what extent does regional policy meet the policy goals of redistribution and overall growth?
- How do types of policy differ in terms of their respective effectiveness?
- Which other determinants of effectiveness can be identified?
- How can future research be designed such that policy relevance is assured?

In this chapter, we first summarise the findings of the literature survey. Then, we present some recent findings on the effectiveness of EU policies. Finally, we draw conclusions and present recommendations for policy and research.

3.1.1 Scope

This contribution is spatially limited to Dutch national and EU policy aimed at specific regions in developed countries. With the exception of the Netherlands, we focus on publications in international, peer-reviewed journals. Moreover, we have concentrated on studies published after 1970 providing quantitative ex post estimations of effectiveness. The post-1970 period is particularly interesting because unemployment was experienced throughout this period as a serious and persistent problem for which regional policy was perceived as a promising solution. In terms of policy instruments, we focus on subsidies and government investments.

3.2 Approach

In a first step, tag words and expert suggestions have been employed to find about 200 possibly interesting studies. From this group of studies, a selection was made, filtering the number of studies down to 54. The following criteria were used:

- Was policy aimed at regional stimulation to decrease lagging welfare development of selected regions or enhancing national economic growth?
- Was concrete policy evaluated? Publications describing solely spatial developments or policy changes without analysis of the effectiveness of policy measures have not been selected.

The literature study was aimed at obtaining aggregated information on the effectiveness of regional policy. In order to be able to aggregate the information from the studies, an estimate has been made of the effectiveness that follows from each study. This effectiveness score is displayed in a figure between 1 (hardly effective) to 5 (very effective). To be sure, in such estimates, a certain degree of subjectivity is unavoidable. We do not pretend to have valued the individual scores that follow from the studies correctly in every individual case. But the expectation is justified that the average scores provide a reasonable impression of the general effectiveness of regional policies.

3.2.1 Research Quality

The evaluated studies have been valued on their research quality. The central question in this respect was if the effectiveness assessment was sufficiently based on sound analysis and arguments. Only 17 out of 54 studies were assessed as useful. Two sorts of limitations led to negative scores. First, many studies ascribe temporal developments to new or changed policies without correcting for autonomous changes such as the business cycle or long-term trends (e.g., Moore and Rhodes 1973; Begg et al. 1976; Schmid and Peters 1982). Second, some studies present gross policy output as policy effects (Wren 1987; ERAC et al. 2003, 2004; several Dutch studies, see below). Gross policy output can be defined as the size of subsidised investment, the total number of subsidised jobs or the production following from subsidised activities. However, in 50–75% of subsidised investments, it turns out that these investments would have taken place without the subsidy as well (Schmid 1979; Swales 1997; Bureau Buiten et al. 2003). For effectiveness measurement purposes, gross policy output is only an upper bound. Relevant are net policy effects: effects that would not have occurred without the evaluated policy. Again, we do not claim complete objectivity with regard to the assessment of the quality of individual studies. However, we think that the positively regarded studies provide better views of effectiveness than the studies that were declined.

3.3 Results

The effectiveness score is 3.3 on average. This score applies to the overall study sample of 54 as well as for the positively regarded subset of studies. However, the spread is large.

Article I: policy goals
The evaluated policies are predominantly aimed at decreasing regional economic differences within countries. Investigated effects are typically growth or employment in the stimulated region. Effects on national welfare are usually not taken into account.[1] The effectiveness of policies with regard to this more broad policy goal is relatively small, both for the total sample of studies as for the positively valued studies. Some studies analyse effectiveness in terms of rather specific policy goals, such as relocating firms and investments to stimulated regions.

[1] Regional policy in the Netherlands aims not only at decreasing regional disparities but at stimulating overall welfare too.

Table 3.1 Policy effectiveness by type of policy instrument

	Average effectiveness	
	All publications	Positively regarded publications
Subsidies	3.4 (15)	3.7 (6)
European regional policy	3.2 (10)	1.9 (3)
General regional policy	3.6 (17)	3.6 (6)

Source: Bijvoet and Koopmans (2004)

Article II: policy instruments
Table 3.1 presents the estimated effectiveness per type of policy instrument. Subsidies seem to have been reasonably successful, but the spread is large. The cohesion fund is the main part of European regional policy. This policy appears fairly successful in the table (3.2), but studies suggesting high effectiveness scores are judged to be of poor scientific quality. More reliable research such as that by CPB (2002a, b) points at lower effectiveness (1.9).

"General regional policy" concerns mainly British research during the 1970s (Moore and Rhodes 1976a, b; Ashcroft and Taylor 1977) investigating three instruments: the system of allowances called Industrial Development Certificate (IDC) and the subsidy measures Investment Incentives and Regional Employment Premium (REP). Generally, these policy instruments have been studied jointly and appear to have been reasonably successful. Within its group of policy instruments, the IDC is regarded by various authors as the most effective.

3.3.1 Research Methods

A chronology can be observed in the application of research methods for regional policy evaluation, starting with shift-and-share analysis throughout the 1970s. Shortly afterwards, regression analysis became both an independent method and a support tool for determining expected values in shift-and-share analysis. During the 1980s, modelling and simulations gained ground. In recent years, existing methods were improved, simultaneous to the application of new methods such as cost–benefit analysis (Swales 1997).

Effectiveness is evaluated positively in many studies by applying shift-and-share analysis and/or model simulations. For regression analysis, the score is somewhat less positive, while high effectiveness is perceived by studies applying surveys and interviews. This is not surprising; the latter sort of research typically entails inquiring entrepreneurs who received grants or subsidies for investments about the impact of policy. The objectiveness of the response in these cases can be influenced by strategic answers. Therefore, we have not valued this kind of studies positively.

Remarkably, during the 1970s, research focused exclusively on macro and regional scales. Only in the late 1980s and 1990s, attention appears to have widened to inclusion of the effects on the micro-level (see for example Wren and Waterson

1991). Micro-level research often shows positive effectiveness scores and is usually of good research quality.

Article III: Dutch policy
The effectiveness of the Dutch investment premium measure (IPR) appears high at first sight (4.3). However, these scores are given by studies whose quality is doubtful. Often gross effects are presented instead of net effects (Moret Ernst & Young 1995; NIBConsult 1998; Bureau Bartels 2003a, b). Many research authors seem to have ignored the favourable economic climate of the 1990s in regional economic performance, classifying such autonomous circumstances as part of policy effects (Moret Ernst & Young 1995; NIBConsult 1998).

In 2003, a midterm review of the 'Compass for the North' was carried out by Ecorys (2003a). The Compass represents a regional economic development program for the lagging northern part of the Netherlands from 2000 until 2006. The study distinguishes three types of non-additional effects:

1. *Deadweight*: the extent to which effects would have manifested without the Compass programme.
2. *Displacement*: the degree to which project effects crowd out investment in other geographical areas within and outside of the northern Netherlands.
3. *Substitution*: the degree to which project effects crowd out additional economic activity in other firms and sectors within the northern Netherlands.

The study pretends to correct for these effects but manages to do so only partly.[2] The employment effect for 2003 (halfway the execution of the program) was estimated at 4.510 fte. This was described as net created employment. Looking at the partial correction for deadweight and other non-additional effects, this estimate probably represents an overestimation. Identical limitations apply to a midterm evaluation of another project within the Compass program (Ecorys 2003b). Ecorys points at the large additional effort required to arrive at further corrections to the gross effects.

Article IV: EU policy
Various estimates of the effects of EU policy differ considerably. Nevertheless, the overall picture can be concluded to be rather negative. Guisan, Cancelo and Diaz (1998) investigated investment subsidies by the European Commission for Research and Development in 103 European regions. By means of a regression analysis, they conclude that investment in R&D influence gross regional product positively.

CPB Netherlands Bureau for Economic Policy Analysis (CPB 2002a) provides an overview of earlier research into the effects of cohesion policy on economic convergence between member states. From this overview, it follows that the median impact of a subsidy of 1% of GDP of a member state equals 0.15% additional annual growth. Every euro of European cohesion subsidy crowds out 17 eurocents

[2] For the firm location policies (one third of the total employment effect), deadweight and substitution effects are not estimated (p. 143). For measures aimed at firms (over half of the total employment effect), there is a correction for deadweight, but not for displacement and substitution (p. 145).

of national stimulation. CPB (2002b) also estimated the effects of the structural funds within the cohesion policy using panel data analysis for 13 countries. The structural funds turn out to exert little influence in enhancing GDP.

ERAC et al. (2003, 2004) investigate the effects of the structural funds over the 1994–1999 period, and the effects of the European Fund for Regional Development (EFRD) between 1975 and 1999. According to these reports the structural funds have resulted in 120,000 jobs during the 1994–1999 period, while the EFRD has realized about 100,000 jobs between 1984 and 1999. These estimates are based on different sources, including estimates made by the beneficiaries of EFRD policy. Sometimes gross effects are estimated, while in other cases, it remains unclear how effects were calculated (ERAC et al. 2003, p. 24). Moreover, ERAC et al. present figures which indicate some degree of convergence between lagging regions and rather prospering regions. It remains unclear whether this convergence is the effect of European policy or of autonomous developments.

3.4 Recent Developments

Six years after our literature study, a brief scan of recent literature on EU policies shows that there is still discussion on research methods and results. Two authors who work at the European Commission are very pessimistic: "*a general lesson which can be drawn from the literature is that it is very difficult, if not altogether impossible, to quantify the part of the observed regional trends that can be attributed to cohesion policy*" (De Michelis and Monfort 2008). Bachtler and Gorzelak (2007) observe that many of the conclusions based on econometric models are hedged with caveats concerning the assumptions made by the models and the data used. They also point to research which has questioned the contribution of cohesion policy to convergence. Begg (2010) states that after more than 20 years of cohesion policy, the evidence remains thin on what has been achieved and that there are heated disputes about whether or not cohesion policy is worthwhile. Begg (2008) also concludes that econometric studies – broadly – offer little support for the contention that cohesion policy is effective. Modelling exercises tend to be more positive, but it is the survey-based assessments that seem to be most sanguine. We note that this chapter argues that econometric (regression) studies are the preferred method, while surveys may generate too optimistic results.

3.5 Conclusions

In 1973, the Expenditures Committee of the British House of Commons stated:

> There must be few areas of Government expenditure in which so much is spent but so little known about the success of the policy…Regional policy has been empiricism run mad, a

> game of hit-and-miss, played with more enthusiasm than success...We regret that their efforts have not been better sustained by the proper evaluation of the costs and benefits of policies pursued (Ashcroft 1979).

The picture drawn by our study is less unfortunate than the sketch above for the UK about three decades ago. However, available research in the effects of regional policy in many cases uses overly simple approaches and highly limiting assumptions. Only a small number of studies measure the effects of policy explicitly and in a scientifically adequate manner.

This leads us to the conclusion that evaluations in the literature offer only scant empirical evidence for underpinning policy choices. The conclusions which can be drawn are displayed below. We add to this that our literature research focuses heavily on policy in lagging regions and hence does not include other types of regional policy.

The effectiveness of subsidies differs considerably between studies, varying from strongly positive to downright negative. Frequently, 50–75% of subsidized jobs and investment turn out to be non-additional, so it cannot be related to regional policy. Direct regulation seems the most effective policy instrument, with the British IDC as the prime example.

There are indications for substitution between EU and national subsidies, advancing the question whether national regional policy overlaps with policy by lower bodies of government. This question cannot be answered in a satisfactory way based on the literature study.

The quality of the applied research methods differs to a large extent. Regression analysis (sometimes combined with economic modeling) is an apt way to measure regional policy effectiveness. Micro-level research into the behaviour of individual firms provides a growing body of studies and appears methodologically promising.

3.6 Recommendations

Based on the study, we recommend to investigate policy in a scientifically responsible way. This implies estimating net effects; the difference with gross effects might be very large. Every measure should be assessed separately, since effects can differ enormously between them. Regression analysis, research into revealed behaviour of individual firms and cost–benefit analysis (or cost-effectiveness analysis) are the appropriate methods for ex post analysis. In midterm evaluations, enquiries and investigations into investments can be used, provided the approach is aimed at non biased, net effects. Finally, policy alternatives should be compared in terms of necessary subsidies per additional job or per euro of economic growth. Scientifically, sound ex post evaluations of policies can be used to estimate the effectiveness of similar new policies ex ante, applying a strict definition of similarity.

Table 3.2 Summary of publications: positively regarded studies

Authors	Year	Country	Policy aimed at	Policy instrument	Micro/macro	Type of research	Method	Effectiveness	Scientific quality
Ashcroft and Swales	1982	UK	Regional unemployment differences	Relocating government	Micro	Quantitative	Model simulation	4.0	Positive
Ashcroft and Taylor	1977	UK	Relocation of industrial firms	General	Macro	Quantitative	Regression analysis	3.5	Positive
CPB	2002a	EU	Regional differences	EU Cohesion Fund	Macro	Quantitative	Regression analysis	2.0	Positive
CPB	2002b	EU	Regional differences	EU Structural Funds	Macro	Quantitative	Regression analysis	2.0	Positive
De Bruyne and Van Rompuy	1982	Belgium	Regional differences	Subs-financial	Macro	Quantitative	Model simulation	–	Positive
Faini and Schiantarelli	1987	Scotland	Relocation of industrial firms	General/subsidies	Micro	Quantitative	Reg./model sim.	4.0	Positive
Guisan et al.	1998	EU	Regional welfare differences	EU regional policy	Macro	Quantitative	Regression analysis	1.7	Positive
Keeble	1980	UK	Relocation of industrial firms	Subs-investment	Macro	Quantitative	Regression analysis	3.0	Positive
Kim and Kim	2002	South Korea	Regional differences	Subs-investment	Macro	Quantitative	Model simulation	4.3	Positive
Moore and Rhodes	1976a	UK	Relocation of industrial firms	General	Macro	Quantitative	Regression analysis	4.0	Positive
Moore and Rhodes	1976b	UK	Regional unemployment differences	General/subsidies	Macro	Both	Shift-share/regr.	3.8	Positive
Nelson and Wyzan	1989	Sweden	Regional differences	General	Macro	Quantitative	Regression analysis	3.5	Positive
Nijkamp and Rietveld	1982	General	Regional differences	General	Macro	Quantitative	Model simulation	3.0	Positive
Ravi Kumar	2002	India	Regional differences	Infrastructure	Macro	Quantitative	Regression analysis	4.0	Positive

Schalk and Untiedt	2000	Germany	Regional economic growth	Subs-investment	Macro	Quantitative	Regression analysis	5.0	Positive
Schmid	1979	Germany	Regional unemployment differences	Subs-loonkosten	Macro	Quantitative	Regression analysis	2.0	Positive
Swales	1997	UK	Regional differences	Subs-investment	Macro	Quantitative	CBA	–	Positive
Tyler	1980	UK	Relocation of industrial firms	General	Macro	Quantitative	Regression analysis	4.0	Positive
Wren and Waterson	1991	UK	Employment	Subs-financial	Micro	Quantitative	Reg./model sim.	3.0	Positive
Bell	1986	RSA	Relocation of industrial firms	General	Macro	Qualitative	Desk research	2.0	Negative
Begg et al.	1976	Scotland	Relocation of industrial firms	General	Macro	Qualitative	Shift-Share	–	Negative
Buck and Atkins	1976	UK	Regional unemployment differences	General	Macro	Quantitative	Regression analysis	3.0	Negative
Bureau Bartels	2003a, b	NL	Economic differences	EPD	Macro	Quantitative	Survey	4.0	Negative
Bureau Buiten et al.	2003	NL	Economic differences	EPD	Macro	Quantitative	Survey	2.0	Negative
Coady and Harris	2001	Mexico	Regional income differences	Cash transfers	Macro	Quantitative	Model simulation	3.3	Negative
Courbis	1982	F	Regional differences	General	Macro	Qualitative	Model simulation	3.0	Neg/Pos
Duijn	1975	NL	Regional unemployment differences	General	Macro	Quantitative	Regression analysis	3.0	Negative
Ecorys	2003a	NL	Economic and social differences	D2–EFRO	Macro	Quantitative	Survey	4.0	Negative
Ecorys	2003b, c	NL	Economic differences	EPD	Macro	Quantitative	Survey	4.5	Negative
ERAC et al.	2003	EU	Regional differences	EU Structural Funds	Macro	Both	Several	4.0	Neg/Pos

(continued)

Table 3.2 (continued)

Authors	Year	Country	Policy aimed at	Policy instrument	Micro/ macro	Type of research	Method	Effectiveness	Scientific quality
ERAC et al.	2004	EU	Regional differences	EU Fund (EFRO)	Macro	Both	Several	4.0	Neg/Pos
Fingleton	1989	UK	Relocation of industrial firms	General	Macro	Quantitative	Model simulation	3.0	Negative
Folmer and Oosterhaven	1983	NL	Regional unemployment differences	General	Macro	Quantitative	Model simulation	3.0	Negative
Freebairn	2003	Australia	More equality between regions	General	Macro	Qualitative	Desk research	3.0	Negative
Frost and Spence	1981	UK	Relocation of industrial firms	General	Macro	Qualitative	Desk research	2.0	Negative
Gupta	1973	India	Regional income differences	Five-year plans	Macro	Quantitative	Desk research	3.3	Negative
Hart	1993	UK	Transport investments	Subs-investment	Macro	Qualitative	Desk research	2.0	Negative
Hassink	2002	D/Jap.SK	Regional innovation support systems	Subs-innovation	Macro	Qualitative	Desk research	4.0	Negative
Holzer et al.	1993	US	Higher productivity	Subs-loonkosten	Macro	Quantitative	Regression analysis	4.0	Negative
Jensen-Butler	1991	Denmark	Relocation of industrial firms	Subs-innovation	Macro	Qualitative	Desk research	2.0	Negative
Kyrgianfini and Sefertzi	2003	Greece	Innovative regions	Subs-innovation	Macro	Qualitative	Survey	5.0	Negative
van der Laan	1987	NL	Migration	Migration policy	Macro	Qualitative	Desk research	–	Negative
Learmonth et al.	2003	Scotland	Clustering	Cluster policy	Macro	Both	Model simulation	–	Negative
MacKay	1976	UK	Regional unemployment differences	REP	Macro	Both	Shift-Share/ regr.	2.0	Negative
Moore and Rhodes	1973	UK	Regional unemployment differences	General/ subsidies	Macro	Qualitative	Shift-Share	4.0	Negative

Moore et al.	1982	UK	Relocation of industrial firms	General	Macro	Qualitative	Shift-Share	3.0	Negative
Moret Ernst & Young	1995	NL	Regional differences, growth	IPR	Micro	Qualitative	Survey	4.5	Negative
NIBConsult	1998	NL	Regional differences, growth	IPR	Beide	Quantitative	Survey	4.0	Negative
Schmid and Peters	1982	Germany	Regional unemployment differences	General	Macro	Quantitative	Regression analysis	2.0	Negative
Taylor and Wren	1997	UK	Regional employment differences	General	Macro	Qualitative	Desk research	4.0	Negative
Tervo	1989	Finland	Productivity in lagging regions	Subs-investment	Micro	Qualitative	Model simulation	4.0	Negative
Van Delft and Suyker	1982	NL	Regional unemployment differences	Subs-investment	Macro	Quantitative	Model simulation	3.0	Negative
Wren	1987	England	Employment, new firms	Subsidies/ general	Macro	Qualitative	Survey	2.3	Negative

Source: Bijvoet and Koopmans (2004)

References

Ashcroft B (1979) The evaluation of regional economic policy: the case of the United Kingdom. In: Allen K (ed) Balanced national growth. Lexington Books, Lexington, MA, pp 231–296

Ashcroft B, Swales JK (1982) Estimating the effects of government office dispersal. Reg Sci Urban Econ 12:81–97

Ashcroft B, Taylor J (1977) The movement of manufacturing industry and the effect of regional policy. Oxf Econ Pap 29(1):84–101

Bachtler J, Gorzelak G (2007) Reforming EU cohesion policy. Policy Stud 28:309–326

Bartels B (2003a) Mid-term evaluatie EPD Oost-Nederland. Bureau Bartels, Amersfoort

Bartels B (2003b) Mid-term evaluatie EPD Zuid-Nederland. Bureau Bartels, Amersfoort

Begg I (2008) Subsidiarity in regional policy. In: Gelauff G et al (eds) Subsidiarity and economic reform in Europe. Springer, Berlin, pp 291–310

Begg I (2010) Cohesion or confusion: a policy searching for objectives. J Eur Integr 32:77–96

Begg HM, Lythe CM, Macdonald DR (1976) The impact of regional policy on investment in manufacturing industry: Scotland 1960–71. Urban Stud 13:171–179

Bell T (1986) The role of regional policy in South Africa. J South Afr Stud 12(2):276–292

Bijvoet C, Koopmans C (2004) De effectiviteit van regionaal beleid (The effectiveness of regional policies). Report 751. SEO Economic Research, Amsterdam

Buck TW, Atkins MH (1976) The impact of British regional policies on employment growth. Oxf Econ Pap 28(1):118–132

Bureau Buiten, LEI, TERP Advies (2003) Mid term review: EPD Flevoland 2000–2006. Bureau Buiten, LEI and TERP Advies, Netherlands.

Coady DP, Harris RL (2001) A regional general equilibrium analysis of the welfare impact of cash transfers: an analysis of progresa in Mexico. TMD discussion paper, No. 76. International Food Policy Research Institute, Washington, DC

Courbis R (1982) Measuring effects of French regional policy by means of a regional-national model. Reg Sci Urban Econ 12:59–79

CPB (2002a) Funds and Games: the economics of European cohesion policy. CPB Netherlands Bureau for Economic Policy Analysis, The Hague

CPB (2002b) Fertile soil for structural funds? A panel data analysis of the conditional effectiveness of European cohesion policy. CPB discussion paper, No. 10, CPB Netherlands Bureau for Economic Policy Analysis, The Hague

De Bruyne G, van Rompuy P (1982) The impact of interest subsidies on the interregional allocation of capital: an econometric analysis for Belgium. Reg Sci Urban Econ 12:121–138

De Michelis N, Monfort P (2008) Some reflections concerning GDP, regional convergence and European cohesion policy. Reg Sci Policy Prac 1:15–22

Duijn JJ (1975) De doelmatigheid van het regionaal-economisch beleid in de jaren zestig. Tijdschr Econ Soc Geogr 66(5):258–271

Ecorys (2003a) Mid-term evaluatie Doelstelling 2-programma Stedelijke Gebieden Nederland 2000–2006. Ecorys, Rotterdam

Ecorys (2003b) Mid term review Kompas voor het Noorden. Ecorys-NEI, Rotterdam

Ecorys (2003c) Mid term evaluatie EPD D2 Noord-Nederland. Ecorys-NEI, Rotterdam

ERAC, IPO, PMN, UvT (2003) Analyse effecten Structuurfondsprogramma's in Nederland, periode 1994–1999. European Regional Affairs Consultants, Boxtel

ERAC, IPO, PMN, UvT (2004) 25 Jaar Europees Fonds voor de Regionale Ontwikkeling (EFRO), in Nederland. European Regional Affairs Consultants, Boxtel

Faini R, Schiantarelli F (1987) Incentives and investment decisions: the effectiveness of regional policy. Oxf Econ Pap 39(3):516–533

Fingleton B (1989) Evaluating British government regional policy: a cost oriented approach. Trans Inst Br Geogr 14(4):446–460, New Series

Folmer H, Oosterhaven J (1983) Measurement of employment effects of Dutch regional socio-economic policy. In: Kuklinski A, Lambooy JG (eds) Dilemmas in regional policy. Mouton, Berlin, New York, Amsterdam, pp 245–270

Freebairn J (2003) Economic policy for rural and regional Australia. Aust J Agric Res Econ 47(3):389–414

Frost M, Spence N (1981) Policy responses to urban and regional economic change in Britain. Geogr J 147(3):321–341

Guisan C, Cancelo T, Diaz R (1998) Evaluation of the effects of European regional policy in the diminution of regional disparities. Working paper of the Euro-American association of economic development, No. 29. European Regional Science Association, Vienna

Gupta S (1973) The role of the public sector in reducing regional income disparity in Indian plans. J Dev Stud 9(3):243–261

Hart T (1993) Transport investment and disadvantaged regions: UK and European policies since the 1950s. Urban Stud 30(2):417–436

Hassink R (2002) Regional innovation support systems: recent trends in Germany and East Asia. Eur Plan Stud 10(2):153–164

Holzer HJ, Block RN, Cheathem M, Knott JH (1993) Are training subsidies for firms effective? The Michigan experience. Ind Labor Relat Rev 46(4):625–636

Jensen-Butler C (1991) Rural industrialisation in Denmark and the role of public policy. Urban Stud 29(6):881–904

Keeble DE (1980) Industrial decline, regional policy and the urban–rural manufacturing shift in the United Kingdom. Environ Plan 12:945–962

Kim E, Kim K (2002) Impacts of regional development strategies on growth and equity of Korea: a multiregional CGE model. Ann Reg Sci 36:165–180

Kyrgianfini L, Sefertzi E (2003) Changing regional systems of innovation in Greece: the impact of regional innovation strategy initiatives in peripheral areas of Europe. Eur Plan Stud 11(8):885–910

Learmonth D, Munro A, Swales JK (2003) Multi-sectoral cluster modelling: the evaluation of Scottish enterprise cluster policy. Eur Plan Stud 11(5):567–584

MacKay RR (1976) The impact of the regional employment premium. In: Withing A (ed) The economics of industrial subsidies. HMSO, London, pp 225–241

Moore BC, Rhodes J (1973) Evaluating the effects of British regional economic policy. Econ J 83(329):87–110

Moore BC, Rhodes J (1976a) Regional economic policy and the movement of manufacturing firms to development areas. Economica 43(169):17–31, New Series

Moore BC, Rhodes J (1976b) A quantitative analysis of the effects of the regional employment premium and other regional policy instruments. In: Withing A (ed) The economics of industrial subsidies. HMSO, London, pp 191–219

Moore BC, Rhodes J, Tyler P (1982) Urban/rural shift and the evaluation of regional policy. Reg Sci Urban Econ 12:139–157

Moret Ernst & Young (1995) De effectiviteit van de IPR. Moret Ernst & Young, Utrecht

Nelson MA, Wyzan ML (1989) Public policy, local labor demand and migration in Sweden, 1979–84. J Reg Sci 29(2):247–264

NIBConsult (1998) Evaluatie besluit subsidies regionale investeringsprojecten. NIBConsult, Den Haag

Nijkamp P, Rietveld P (1982) Measurement of the effectiveness of regional policies by means of multiregional economic models. In: Issaev B, Nijkamp P, Rietveld P, Snickars F (eds) Multiregional economic modelling: practice and prospect. North-Holland Publishing Company, Amsterdam, pp 65–81

Ravi Kumar T (2002) The impact of regional infrastructure investment in India. Reg Stud 36(2):194–200

Schalk HJ, Untiedt G (2000) Regional investment incentives in Germany: impacts on factor demand and growth. Ann Reg Sci 34:173–195

Schmid G (1979) The impact of selective employment policy: the case of a wage-cost subsidy scheme in Germany 1974–1975. J Ind Econ 27(4):339–358

Schmid G, Peters AB (1982) The German federal employment program for regions with special employment problems: an evaluation. Reg Sci Urban Econ 12:99–119

Swales K (1997) A cost–benefit approach to the evaluation of regional selective assistance. Fisc Stud 18(1):73–85

Taylor J, Wren C (1997) UK regional policy: an evaluation. Reg Stud 31(9):835–848
Tervo H (1989) A micro-level approach to the analysis of the displacement effects of regional incentive policy: the case of Finland. Reg Stud 23(6):511–521
Tyler P (1980) The impact of regional policy on a prosperous region: the experience of the West Midlands. Oxf Econ Pap 32(1):151–162, New Series
Van Delft A, Suyker WBC (1982) Regional investment subsidies: an estimation of the labour market effects for the Dutch regions. Pap Reg Sci Assoc 49:151–168
van der Laan L (1987) Residential migrations and Spatial policies in mixed economies, a case study of the Dutch Randstad. Trans Inst Br Geogr 12(1):84–96, New Series
Wren C (1987) The relative effects of local authority financial assistance policies. Urban Stud 24:268–278
Wren C, Waterson M (1991) The direct employment effects of financial assistance to industry. Oxf Econ Pap 43(1):116–138

Chapter 4
Ex Post Evaluation of Rotterdam Port Investment

Bart Kuipers and Wouter Jonkhoff

Abstract The paper describes Rotterdam post-war port policy making, exploring the policy background for investment in the large-scale Maasvlakte 1 port area. The description is followed by an ex post evaluation of investment in Maasvlakte 1 over the 1968–2002 period. The ex post costs and benefits of the investment provide new insights on the presumption of the Maasvlakte 1 harbour area within the port of Rotterdam as a "cash cow" with a view to current investment to enlarge the port area by constructing Maasvlakte 2.

Keywords Maasvlakte 1 • Maasvlakte 2 • Port facilities • Port investment • Rotterdam

4.1 Introduction

September 2008 saw the "first splash"; the start of construction of Maasvlakte 2 in the port of Rotterdam harbour area. Maasvlakte 2, located next to Maasvlakte 1, forms a westward extension of the port into the North Sea. Maasvlakte 2 represents, similar to the dedicated Betuweroute rail connection between the port of Rotterdam and the German hinterland, a major investment directed at increasing the port's cargo handling capacity and at new investment opportunities for port-based industries. This investment entails the development of extensive harbour territory related to the development of large-scale transport and logistics infrastructure. Such development has been the dominant port strategy of most major seaports in Western Europe (Kuipers 2003) and appears similar to the development of the port of Rotterdam in the 1950s and 1960s in which Maasvlakte 1 was created.

B. Kuipers (✉)
Erasmus School of Economics, Erasmus University Rotterdam, P.O. Box 1738, 3000 DR Rotterdam, The Netherlands
e-mail: bkuipers@ese.eur.nl

W. Manshanden and W. Jonkhoff (eds.), *Infrastructure Productivity Evaluation*, SpringerBriefs in Economics 1, DOI 10.1007/978-1-4419-8101-1_4,

Considering this repetitive way of investing in port facilities, it appears useful to evaluate to what degree Maasvlakte 2's predecessor, Maasvlakte 1, has met prior expectations set by policymakers. Negative public opinion arose after the Maasvlakte 1 infrastructure was completed. Maasvlakte 1 has been described the "failure of the century" because large parts of the area remained empty after the completion of the project since port development in Rotterdam stagnated since the 1970s. Why, then, has Maasvlakte 1 been constructed? Does Maasvlakte 1 set an example of successful or failed policy making and is it possible to arrive at a useful evaluation after 40 years of operation? A prior ex post evaluation of Maasvlakte 1 appears not to have been carried out.

This contribution attempts to evaluate ex post, taking policy considerations as the starting point. Next, the development of Maasvlakte 1 in the 35-year period after completion is described. Finally, conclusions are drawn on the effectiveness and efficiency of the investment. The most comprehensive source used to get a view to policy practice in the 1960s and 1970s is De Goey (1990). However, we commence by providing an introduction on the relevance of performing ex post evaluations.

4.2 Ex Post Evaluation of Infrastructure Projects: Too Little, Too Late?

The usual starting point for Dutch infrastructure evaluations is the so-called OEI leidraad guidelines. This acronym stands for Overview of Effects of Infrastructure. These guidelines are the "Dutch book of etiquette" for infrastructure investment evaluation (Eijgenraam et al. 2000). However, they provide no coverage of ex post evaluation. Only recently, Berveling et al. (2009) have expressed the need for conducting ex post evaluation. They state four reasons for the lack of interest in ex post evaluations. First, the desire to look ahead is a key factor in the political-administrative and policy context: policymakers are by nature focused on the future, not on the past. Second, certain psychological processes can render one disinclined to pursue evaluations. An "optimism bias" can play a role at the start of a project, meaning that those involved (ex ante) often have overly optimistic views about a project. Negative evaluations can damage a person's professional reputation. The third reason is related to different organisational barriers, like the ending of project teams, lack of funding, organisational capacity, and so on. Finally and most importantly, Berveling et al. (2009) mention methodological problems. It is not only difficult to isolate the effects of a particular project but also to envision what the world would be like had that project not been commissioned. In addition, the timing of evaluation is an issue that demands particular attention.

The observations by Berveling et al. (2009) are particularly relevant for an ex post evaluation of Maasvlakte 1. The decision to invest in Maasvlakte 1 was made in the late 1960s, a period characterised by continuous growth of global trade and foreign direct investment. During the 1970s, both the external environment of the port of Rotterdam as well as priorities underlying policy making in the city of Rotterdam changed dramatically. Berveling et al. (2009) restrict their analysis to so-called line infrastructure like roads, instead of "point infrastructure" like ports or business parks. They state a period of 3 years after the opening of an infrastructural project as the optimal time span for the ex post evaluation, being able to take into account so-called ingrowth effects. Evaluations after longer time spans are frequently disrupted by new developments like the effects of other infrastructures or changes in the economic situation. After multiple decades, society will have changed to such a degree that existing infrastructure is "embedded" in present-day society's functioning. Hence, it is hardly possible to isolate the effects of historical investments.

Three years may be the optimal period for the ex post evaluation of line infrastructure. An important characteristic of most new roads is the fact that the new capacity should relieve capacity problems on related highways in the network and therefore will generate traffic from the start of the project. New stretches of road infrastructure solve bottlenecks in a usually heavily used network. By contrast, the demand for space in seaports or business parks is not connected to a "fluid network" like urban road networks. Large seaport areas usually take many years to be filled. The demand for space is characterised by irregular demand fluctuations. These fluctuations are the reason behind the phased or flexible construction of large port projects. A seaport project usually starts accommodating the arrival of a launching customer (CPB et al. 2001b). Therefore, 3 years seems much too short for ex post evaluation of a large investment project like the first (or second) Maasvlakte.

A number of objections to ex post evaluations have been presented. Should we then conclude that ex post evaluation of infrastructure projects is merely an interesting intellectual experiment? On the contrary, ex post evaluation of infrastructure is considered useful because it offers the opportunity to learn from the past. First, applying comparisons of ex post evaluations to ex ante evaluations can help to check whether necessary assumptions underlying ex ante evaluations have been correct.[1] Comparing between ex ante and ex post evaluations enables one to assess and improve transport and other models applied or to produce meta-evaluations by comparing different types of infrastructure projects.

Second, by producing an ex post evaluation it is possible to assess responsibility for the project – was the investment well-considered from a financial or societal point of view? (Berveling et al. 2009). In addition, knowledge of real developments and financial history of investment projects can enrich the rather mechanistic practice of extrapolating ex ante evaluations. A similar way of reasoning applies to welfare effects outside the transport market. The indirect effects on markets other than the transport market receive increased societal interest, possibly because of the shock-wise nature of the effects of infrastructure investment outside the transport market – be its effects on the labour market, price development of real estate or traffic generating effects. These effects receive increased attention by policymakers and can be modelled in spatial computable general equilibrium models (SCGEs).[2]

---

[1] Relevant examples include the (rejected) second national Dutch airport and the Delta waterworks in the south western Oosterschelde area (Ministerie van Financiën 1986).

[2] See Kuipers et al. (2003) for an illustration of seaport investment evaluation with the Dutch spatial computable general equilibrium model RAEM.

It seems fair to conclude that the value of ex post evaluation for decision making exceeds the level of intellectual experiments. A possible reason for the absence of ex post evaluation in decision making, then, is the fragmentary nature of responsibilities in the public domain. Dutch policy practice is illustrative. Ex ante evaluation is the natural domain of the ministry of Economic Affairs and the related Central Planning Bureau, while ex post evaluation is predominantly carried out by organisations occupied with regular performance monitoring. In the Netherlands, this strand of evaluation is mostly the domain of the ministry of Finance and the Court of Audit (Algemene Rekenkamer) (Ministerie van Financiën 2002).

4.3 Three Criteria for Ex Post Evaluation

Ex post evaluation monitors policy with regard to achievement of objectives, effectiveness and efficiency (Ministerie van Financiën 2002). *Achievement of objectives* deals with the extent to which intended effects of policy measures are being achieved. Related to the Maasvlakte 1 port area: "What was the purpose of policy for which construction of the Maasvlakte 1 was instrumental?", and: "Were the intended effects of the Maasvlakte 1 realised?" *Effectiveness* deals with the extent to which intended effects are realised due to the executed policy. Is there a connection between the allocated resources and achieving the desired policy goals? *Efficiency* or cost effectiveness relates the desired effects to resources allocated. Could the desired effects have been realised allocating a smaller amount of resources? Was the cost of approximately 275 million Euros (Weigand 1997) at the time really necessary to realise the desired policy effects of Maasvlakte 1?

The above stresses the importance of policy goals for ex post evaluation. In the following section, we assess the development of Maasvlakte 1 with a view to set policy goals and the extent these were achieved.

4.4 Maasvlakte 1 in Historical Perspective

Post-war Rotterdam port policy was characterised by differing paradigms. Development of Maasvlakte 1 occurred within the framework of post-war development of the port. The expansion of the area began when the Botlek Plan was decided upon in 1947. The second step was the Europoort plan, executed in 1957. Several versions of the Europoort plan contained elements of a so-called Maasvlakte ("Meuse marshland"; Fig. 4.1). Already in 1962 concepts for extending the Europoort area were developed, with the Maasvlakte envisioned to develop southward along the Voorne coast stretch. Between 1950 and 1970 the Rotterdam port area was continuously enlarged, both in terms of released port space and newly constructed space (Fig. 4.2). Investment in the Maasvlakte 1 area started in 1968.

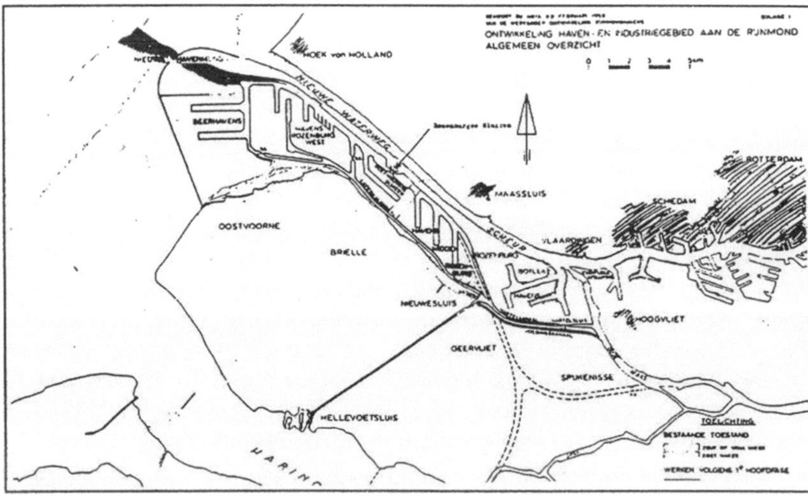

Fig. 4.1 Plan-Europoort according to Werkgroep Ontwikkeling Rijnmondhavens, 1958. *Source*: De Goey (1990)

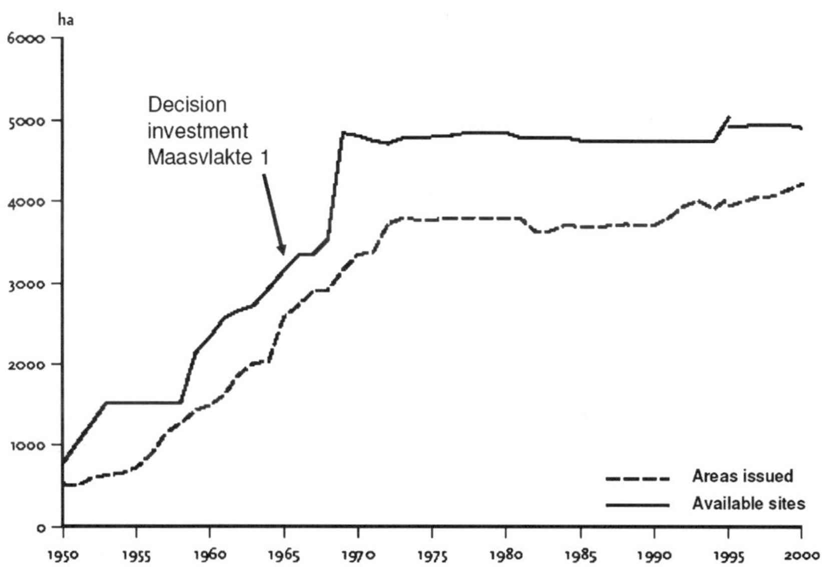

Fig. 4.2 Available and released spaces in the Rotterdam port area, 1950–2000. *Source*: CPB et al. (2001a)

The basic form was completed in 1973 – the full development of Maasvlakte 1, however, was a phased development process during the 1970–1990s.

The port spaces in the Botlek and Europoort areas were predominantly used to locate petrochemical activities. Generally speaking, four determinants were responsible for the rapid growth of industrial clusters in the seaports of Western Europe. First, strong worldwide development of the petrochemical industry (related to the fourth long-term Kondratieff business cycle) saw seaports play an important role in economic geography (Van Duijn 1979). A second factor was the "run to the coast" principle in the location of basic and processing industries after World War II due to – among others – economies of scale in the transport sector (Dicken and Lloyd 1990). Third, US companies directed large amounts of foreign direct investment to Europe. A fourth determinant was the supply of large-scale spaces in seaport areas, developed within the framework of strategic policy goals set by most seaports. All four developments could be observed in the port of Rotterdam, resulting in the development of the largest interconnected industrial area in Europe.

De Goey observes how Rotterdam port policy around 1970 experienced a major shift. He divides notions on port policy principles over two periods, identifying the 1945–1970 period characterised by major expansion of the port area and the post-1970 period without significant expansion.

(a) Figure 4.3
(b) 1945–1970

Throughout the period between 1945 and 1970 the municipality of Rotterdam was the dominant policymaker concerning port policy. The most important goal set

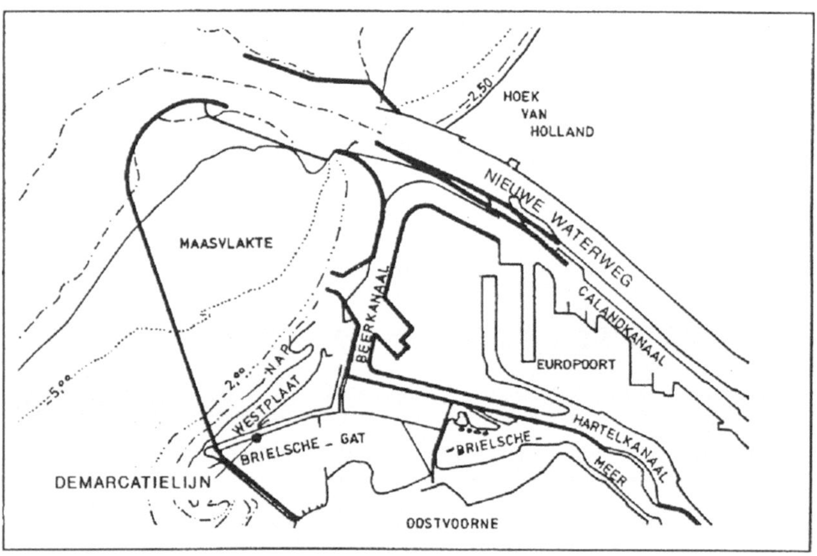

Fig. 4.3 One of the demarcation line variants of Maasvlakte 1. *Source*: De Goey (1990)

by the city council was creating a sufficient amount of employment for the local population. The interest in increasing manufacturing sectors was predominantly one of making the port less dependent on business cycles, especially since the transport function of the port (transit, transport, cargo handling) had traditionally been the most important activity. Industrial development would strengthen the economic base of the region and develop its own demand for goods and inputs. The Rotterdam Municipal Port Management traditionally employed the "tonne-measure" – the number of tonnes of cargo handled in the port – as the selection criterion for investments. Companies generating many tonnes of seaborne cargo were considered seaport-related. Moreover, they provided port fees. However, during the 1960s the investments in the port caused severe shortages on the regional labour market, causing port location policy to shift towards labour extensive manufacturers.

Port expansion fuelled interest by the iron and steel industry (notably Hoesch and Hoogovens) for locating on Maasvlakte 1, fitting the trend of process industry migration to the coast. The additional interest in port spaces by Bayer, Shell Chemicals and an asbestos company forced Rotterdam Municipal Port Management to mark Maasvlakte 1 as completely full before construction had even commenced (De Goey 1990). Eventually Bayer and the asbestos company were refused and Shell Chemicals had to locate in Moerdijk (a port facility thirty kilometres southeast of the port of Rotterdam; see Fig. 4.4). Not surprisingly, plans for construction of a second and third Maasvlakte emerged. De Goey (1990) states that the public debate at the time centred around the theme of demarcating the future borders of the Maasvlakte

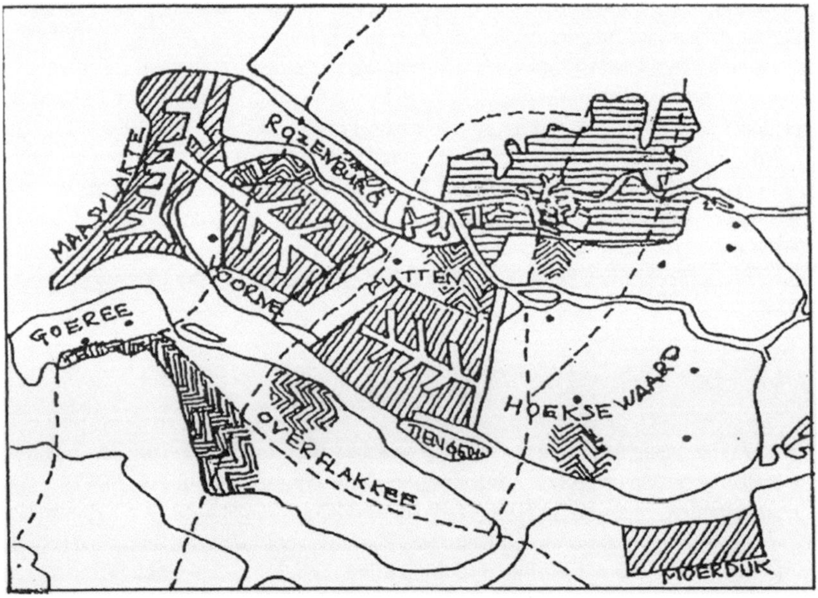

Fig. 4.4 Illustration of the Plan 2000+ in newspaper *Het Vrije Volk*, February 7, 1969. *Source*: De Goey (1990)

area and the exact size and location of a "demarcation line" (Fig. 4.3). Besides tension on the labour market, pressure on the environment was felt, in particular in the vulnerable and valuable coastal dune area south of Maasvlakte 1.

A second major development was the formulation of the "Plan 2000+" by the Rotterdam Municipal Port Management. This plan (Fig. 4.4) can be regarded the culmination of port development in the port of Rotterdam, as it projects the transformation of the complete island of Voorne-Putten into harbour space. The plan caused broad resistance among the citizens of Rotterdam, ending the rapid expansion of the port.

The central goal of creating Maasvlakte 1 had been to contribute to the industrialization of the port, creating employment and regional economic stability, and generating income for the port authority based on shipped tons handled. By 1970, serious pressure was felt on the labour market. Extended expansion of the port would only increase this pressure. In addition, the region's economic stability did not endure, as the effects of five societal shocks to the port indicate.

Around 1970, the large-scale technocratic intentions for port development as formulated in the Plan 2000+ had led to organised resistance among the population of the Rotterdam region (Pinder 1981). Moreover, progressive politics came to rule the city council. This political turnaround put political positions in Rotterdam upside down, damaging the traditional support for port development within the communal board. In October 1970, a period of serious smog was experienced by the population, fuelling existing resistance against further development of the port area. A further influential development was a redesign of national spatial policy towards a spread of population and development of corridor areas directed at stimulating new residential and business areas outside the major cities. In this framework, notably the Selective Investment Regulation ("Selectieve Investeringsregeling") impacted negatively on the development of the port.[3] Last but not least, the oil crisis of 1973 tempered the petrochemical industry's willingness to invest considerably.

After Rotterdam's communal board voted against investments in iron and steel manufacturing locations on the Maasvlakte in 1971, the aforementioned shocks made the community alter its spatial policy, increasing the stress on residential quality within the city's neighbourhoods. Social and urban regeneration became the central imperatives. Port policy lost the priority it had enjoyed during the 1950s and 1960s.

4.4.1 Port Policy After 1970

By 1971, the basic infrastructure of Maasvlakte 1 was finished and the first business investments on Maasvlakte 1 were announced: the construction of V.O.M. (Verenigd Overslagbedrijf Maasvlakte NV), a large dry bulk terminal, and M.O.T. (Maasvlakte Olie Terminal), a large-scale oil terminal. These two initial customers were responsible for 13% of the net available terrains to be rented on Maasvlakte 1.

[3] See the contribution by Manshanden and Dröes in Chap. 5.

Within port policy the stress on stimulating locating seaport-related industry was replaced by fostering the less polluting transport function as well as increasing environmental quality and lowering the pressure on the environment. Other characteristics of the new policy paradigm were a rather unresponsive position of the city council towards newly locating firms in the port and increasing the environmental quality of existing locations. The central government exercised a strongly growing influence on port development. Seaport policy was regionalised: policy became integrally formulated for all of the ports in the Netherlands' Rhine and Meuse delta. A growing number of legal procedures as well as increased stakeholder participation tempered the speed of decision making compared to the prior situation, in which business was done between the city council and a limited number of businessmen related to the harbour. Due to the deterioration of the Rotterdam Municipal Port Management's financial position after the huge investments of the 1950s and 1960s, investment was encouraged which would improve the financial position of the port. Increasing the existing income sources for the port municipality was mostly realised with port dues and rental fees. Instead of using the infrastructure for realising the broad socio-economic development of the port (De Goey 1990), Maasvlakte 1 was now intended as a "cash cow." Finally, the importance of qualitative labour market aspects was stressed, such as jobs demanding specialised education and high wage jobs.

The area, completed in 1973, would locate no industrial companies. Further development of the port of Rotterdam by geographical expansion came to a stop. The 1971–1983 period may be indicated as the first phase in the development of Maasvlakte 1. This phase was characterised by stagnation (Fig. 4.5 and Table 4.1). Only in 1984, another new and important investment project started: the construction of a large-scale container terminal by container stevedoring firm ECT. Over the 35-year history of Maasvlakte 1, ECT became by far the dominant user (Table 4.1).

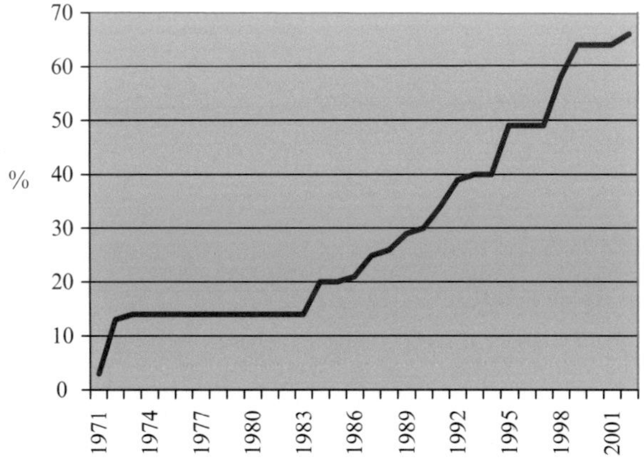

Fig. 4.5 Utilisation rate Maasvlakte 1: 1971–2002 (options excluded). *Source*: Weigand (1997), Port of Rotterdam year reports 1998–2003

Table 4.1 Occupation history Maasvlakte 1: 1971–2002 (options excluded), major investments (>1 hectare) in hectares

	1971	1972	1973	1984	1986	1987	1988	1989	1990	1991	1992	1993	1994	1995	1997	1998	1999	2000	2001	2002	Total
VOM/ EKOM	38							30		32											100
M.O.T.		131																	–8		123
Gasunie			12																		12
ECT				82				6		1	46	3	8	110		28	71				355
RISC					4																4
EZH						56															56
AVR							6														6
NAM							4	3	11				2								20
RISC								1													1
EKOM/ EURO										29	16										45
Eneco											3										3
Ultralight												1									1
Douane															8						8
ARCO/ Lyondell																60					60
Reebok																11					11
Eurofrigo																7					7
EBS																	9				9
Prologis																	8				8
Hankook																		2			2
TOR-line																				20	20
Distripark																				2	2
Yearly totals	38	131	12	82	4	56	10	40	11	62	64	4	10	110	8	106	88	2	–8	22	
Cumulative	38	169	181	263	268	323	334	373	384	446	511	515	525	635	643	749	837	839	831	853	853
As part of net amount of terrains to be rented (%)	3	13	14	20	21	25	26	29	30	34	39	40	40	49	49	58	64	64	64	66	

Source: Weigand (1997), Port of Rotterdam year reports 1998–2003

With the ECT-investment, a second phase in the development of Maasvlakte 1 was initiated: the development of Maasvlakte 1 as a large-scale container-terminal location. During the 1990s, ECT gradually expanded the terminal capacity and by 2002 ECT was responsible for nearly a quarter of total space used on Maasvlakte 1 (Table 4.1). An additional expansion of Maasvlakte 1 emerged in 1985 with the construction of the "Slufter," a depot for polluted mud, for the large part originating from the port basins. This was, however, a public investment, not aimed at "cash cow" goals.

The third phase in the development of Maasvlakte 1 started in 1998 when Arco Chemical (in 1998 bought by Lyondell) started construction of a large-scale chemical plant and when "Distripark Maasvlakte" welcomed its first customers: Reebok, a European Distribution Centre for sports equipment, and Eurofrigo, a cold store. Especially the investment by Arco Chemical was remarkable: it represented an investment contrary to the port policy principles formulated in the early 1970 with respect to the development of Maasvlakte 1.

Thirty-five years after construction started, only 66% of the net available space (853 hectares out of 1,300; see Fig. 4.1) were in use. The rather modest development of Maasvlakte 1 since the early 1970s fits the larger picture of the port of Rotterdam (Fig. 4.2). No dramatic increase of areas issued was observed during those years. Only in the mid-1990s demand started to grow gradually.

4.5 Ex Post Analysis 1968–2002

In the next paragraph, a provisional analysis will be presented based on the costs of construction of Maasvlakte 1 and the benefits of the project. This analysis will be positioned in the broader ex post evaluation framework as suggested by the Dutch ministry of Finance (Ministerie van Financiën 2002), with achievement of objectives, efficiency and effectiveness as the central criteria. The ex ante societal cost–benefit analysis on Maasvlakte 2 evaluates a period of 35 years (CPB et al. 2001a). In this ex post evaluation, we will also take a 35-year period for our analysis because we like to confront the results of the two evaluations, starting with the construction of Maasvlakte 1 in 1968.

4.5.1 Costs

The construction costs of the investment in Maasvlakte 1 consist of three important components. The first is the construction of the "Zuiderdam." The Zuiderdam is the western seawall separating Maasvlakte 1 from the North Sea (see Fig. 4.3). This is an investment in the nautical infrastructure of the port. The Zuiderdam has been constructed to allow the entrance of the largest bulk carriers in the port as a whole and to redirect ocean currents. The Zuiderdam and related nautical infrastructure form the most expensive component of total investment related to Maasvlakte 1. However, this investment serves to improve the accessibility of the port of

Rotterdam as a whole and therefore is not directly related to Maasvlakte 1. Maasvlakte 1 may be considered a "spin-off" of this investment. Because of the nautical character of the Zuiderdam for the total port basin, the majority of the 770 million Dutch guilders (350 million Euro) in the 1965–1968 period has been invested by the Dutch government – some 56%. This investment does not represent a part of the costs of construction of Maasvlakte 1 (Weigand 1997).

The second construction cost component is the actual development of the terrains of Maasvlakte 1, surrounded by the Zuiderdam to the west and the Europoort area to the east (Fig. 4.3). The amount of space needed for commercial use on Maasvlakte 1 has been determined by nautical tests and not by a demand forecast for space needed (Weigand 1997). The cost for construction of the basic infrastructure of Maasvlakte 1 in 1968–1971 amounted to 600 million Dutch guilders (272 million Euro/1.2 billion Euro in 2010) according to Weigand (1997). Overall, the construction costs for Maasvlakte 1 have been relatively low because Maasvlakte 1 is located on a naturally formed sand basin where the sea is already shallow. Moreover, a large amount of sand resulting from, amongst others, the construction of the Europoort plan has been dumped in the sea at the Maasvlakte 1 location.

The third construction cost component is the development of specific port infrastructure on the Maasvlakte for new users like ECT, Lyondell or Distripark Maasvlakte.

The construction costs of Maasvlakte 1 increased because of a number of specific investments – the third cost issue – notably, the large-scale investment in dedicated facilities for deep sea container terminals for ECT and APMT and dedicated investment for the Lyondell facility. The investment history and related financial consequences for the large-scale deep sea container infrastructure on Maasvlakte 1 have been described in detail by Weigand (1999). An important issue in the investment in container infrastructure is the difference in investment in "basic infrastructure" and "infrastructure-plus." Basic infrastructure refers to investment in a port basin and quays. Infrastructure-plus refers to parts of the supra-structure of the terminals, such as pipelines, tracks for container cranes, offices, warehouses, etc. This investment is usually the responsibility of the user of the terminal, but the Port of Rotterdam Authority made public–private arrangements. Weigand (1999) has presented financial statistics for both the basic infrastructure and infrastructure-plus. For the sake of clarity and comparability we present the figures on basic infrastructure (Table 4.2).

In addition to the three construction cost components, we also included the maintenance costs.

The total costs for investment in the basic infrastructure of Maasvlakte 1 for the 1968–2002 period amount to 1.481 million Dutch guilders. By using the historical inflation rate,[4] we transferred the investment figures presented in Table 4.2 to Euro prices for 2010. Because we used historical prices, we did not use a time preference related to the real interest rate, assuming there is no alternative allocation of invested capital. This exercise resulted in a total cumulative investment in the basic Maasvlakte 1 infrastructure for 1968–2002 period of 1.8 billion Euro (2010 prices).

[4] Source: Statistics Netherlands, http://statline.cbs.nl/statweb/

Table 4.2 Cost elements in the construction of basic infrastructure of Maasvlakte 1, 1968–2002, in million Dutch guilders (current prices), Zuiderdam excluded

Cost element	Investment	Period
0. Zuiderdam	770	1965–1968
1. Maasvlakte 1	600	1968–1971
2. Specific port infrastructure:		
Basic infrastructure for large-scale container terminal development		
(a) DMU terminal	103	1982–1987
(b) Connection area	92	1989–1995
(c) Plan Delta 2000-8	250	1993–2000
Distripark Maasvlakte	100	1996–1996
Arco/Lyondell	280	1995–1999
3. Maintenance	56	1971–2002
Total: 1+2+3	1481	1968–2002

Source: Weigand (1997); Weigand (1999); Port of Rotterdam year reports 1998–2004

4.5.2 Benefits

The benefits consist of four main components:

- Port charges for deep sea and inland shipping
- Benefits from land lease
- Quay dues
- Property and other taxes

In addition, Maasvlakte 1 generates added value, employment and a number of other indirect benefits. However, we limit ourselves to direct and priced benefits. A detailed picture of the benefits is lacking because of the confidentiality of these figures. So we estimated the benefits by integrating the available information into one time series. Weigand (1997) presents the benefits of Maasvlakte 1 in terms of the four direct items mentioned above for 1995 in detail. Information on 1968–1975 is present for the total costs and benefits of Maasvlakte 1.[5] Also, Weigand (1999) presents the costs and benefits for the container segment on Maasvlakte 1 in detail. In addition, we found information on two additional years in financial year reports in the port archive of the Port of Rotterdam. To present an estimation, we combined these sources and used two determinants for the level of benefits, first the utilisation rate of Maasvlakte 1 (Fig. 4.5) and second the pattern of port throughput in 1968–2003. In this pattern, we paid particular attention to statistics with respect to coal, ore, crude oil and containers because throughput related figures explain the benefits of Maasvlakte 1 up to 60 or 70%.

When confronting costs and benefits related to Maasvlakte 1, peaks in investment become clear: a first peak in constructing Maasvlakte 1 in 1968–1971 and a

[5] Source: personal archive of a former director of the Port of Rotterdam Authority, available at the Municipality of Rotterdam archive.

second peak starting in the mid-1990s when the large-scale container infrastructure and investment for the Lyondell facility in basic port infrastructure was undertaken (see Fig. 4.6). The benefits are related to the large bulk terminals and start to grow in the early 1990s because of the strong growth of the container throughput. Total benefits amount to 2.3 billion Euro (constant prices of 2010). Confronting these benefits with the costs of constructing the basic port infrastructure of Maasvlakte 1 results in total benefits of 0.6 billion Euro (prices of 2010, see Table 4.3).

The internal rate of return (IRR) appears very modest with only 1.8%. If related to a real efficiency requirement of 8% (CPB et al. 2001a), Maasvlakte 1 has not been the intended cash cow for the Port of Rotterdam. Including the Zuiderdam in the calculation, the result is clearly negative because the construction of this seawall increases costs by 1.5 billion Euro.

To be sure, two important issues have not been not included so far: the residual value of Maasvlakte 1 and its contribution to the users of the port. These two issues are very relevant since they represent the two dominant benefits in the ex ante cost–benefit analysis of Maasvlakte 2 (CPB et al. 2001a, b).

We expect a very significant residual value. First, after 2002 additional investment took place on Maasvlakte 1, resulting in an expansion of the deep sea container infrastructure. Second, rapid growth of the container segment in the years 2002–2008

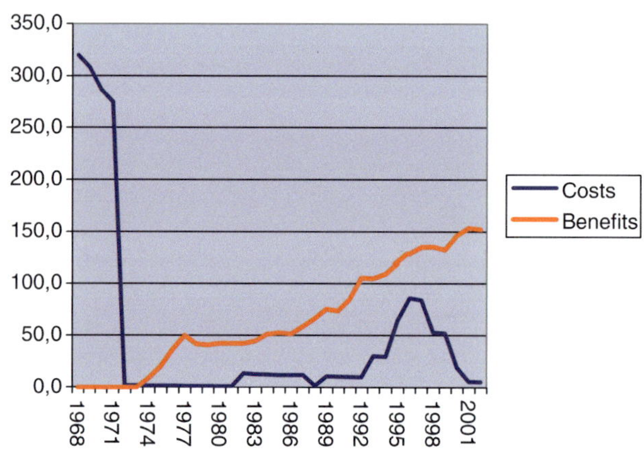

Fig. 4.6 Cost and benefits of Maasvlakte 1, 1968–2002, in million euro (2010 prices)

Table 4.3 Costs and benefits and internal rate of return of the construction of Maasvlakte 1, 1968–2002, million Euro, prices of 2010

Total costs	1,753
Total benefits	2,306
Result	553
IRR	1.8%

in the port of Rotterdam results in a spectacular growth of benefits. In 2002 3.8 million TEU containers were handled at Maasvlakte 1 while, at the peak in 2008, 7.9 million TEU were handled. The growth in container throughput on Maasvlakte 1 exceeds the expectations of the Port of Rotterdam Authority in 1999 (Weigand 1999) by far – including the effects of the crisis in 2009. Third, next to the growth of containers additional investment has been realised on Maasvlakte 1 such as a large palm-oil refinery and second large-scale coal-fired power plant. This resulted in full occupation of Maasvlakte 1 in 2010. Starting from a conservative approach by using the latest benefit calculated for 2002 as a proxy, a discount rate of 2.5% and a risk premium of 0.03, the residual value is estimated at about 2.7 billion Euro – a much higher residual value compared to the 1.0 billion calculated for Maasvlakte 2 in the most optimistic scenario (CPB et al. 2001b).

4.5.3 *Maasvlakte 1 and 2: Ex Post and Ex Ante Results Compared*

When comparing basic figures for Maasvlakte 1 and 2 (Table 4.4), three important observations spring to mind. First, the construction of Maasvlakte 1 was considered fairly inexpensive – only 600 million Dutch guilders. However, when expressed in Euros of 2010 (1.2 billion), Maasvlakte 1 appeared a more sizeable investment project compared to Maasvlakte 2. Second, the exploitation result of Maasvlakte 1 has been more positive than that for Maasvlakte 2. This is unexpected because of two decades of very poor occupation of Maasvlakte 1. The most satisfactory explanation relates to the seawall that is included in the calculations for Maasvlakte 2

Table 4.4 Costs and benefits of Maasvlakte 1 and 2, 35 years after starting investment, in billion Euros of 2010 (Maasvlakte 1) and 2000 (Maasvlakte 2)

	Maasvlakte 1	Maasvlakte 2
Exploitation		
Investment in basic infrastructure	−1.2	−1.1
of which seawall	(−1.5)	−0.6
Balance: investment and exploitation	0.5	−0.9
Effects on users of the port		
Containers	0.3	0.6
Chemicals	0.0	0.1
Other users	0.0	−0.1
External effects	n.a.	−0.1
Indirect effects	n.a.	0.0
Subtotal after 35 years	0.8	−0.3
Residual value	2.7	1.0
Total	3.5	0.8

Source: Maasvlakte 1: own calculations, Maasvlakte 2: CPB et al. (2001b). Maasvlakte 1: seawall excluded. Maasvlakte 2: Global Competition scenario, start of construction in 2010

and excluded for Maasvlakte 1. In addition, an important issue that hardly received attention in the cost–benefit analysis relates to shifting flows of containerised cargo between Maasvlakte 1 and 2. Important customers of ECT are investing in terminal capacity on Maasvlakte 2 and will shift containers from Maasvlakte 1 to Maasvlakte 2. In our cost–benefit setting, this implies an increase in the exploitation effects of Maasvlakte 2 and a decrease of the residual value of Maasvlakte 1. The third observation is the difference in the total effect of Maasvlakte 1 and 2. Of course, including the seawall would also result in a negative total effect for Maasvlakte 1. However, the residual value of Maasvlakte 1 is much more positive compared to Maasvlakte 2. Based on very positive assumptions, the residual value of Maasvlakte 1 also could be 5–7 billion Euro. In addition to the very conservative determined exploitation value, the estimated residual value of Maasvlakte 2 seems inexplicably low.

An additional observation is related to the time-distribution effects of Maasvlakte 1. Even after two decades of very low occupation (Fig. 4.5), the container boom of the 1990s resulted in a positive result of the cost–benefit calculation – especially with the inclusion of the residual value.

What does this tell us about legitimacy, effectiveness and efficiency? To what extent have policy objectives been met, what is the level of effectiveness and what is the level of efficiency related to public projects like large-scale seaport investment projects?

The original policy objectives in the late 1960s were related to a stable socio-economic development of the port of Rotterdam by means of investment in the industrial function of the port. After 1970 these policy goals were adjusted towards development of the less polluting transport function, combined with the need to increase the environmental quality of the port and improvement of the financial situation of the port. Maasvlakte 1 had to act as a cash cow for the port. In general, these objectives were met. Investment in Maasvlakte 1 was indeed characterised by the transport function. The large liquid and dry bulk terminals, as well as the large-scale container terminals are examples of labour extensive operations, producing only modest levels of negative externalities compared to the port-related oil and chemical industry. The actual development of Maasvlakte 1 could be strongly related to policy decisions and the political climate in the port of Rotterdam during the early 1970s.

The second criterion was effectiveness. Was there a connection between the allocated resources and achieving the desired policy goals? Considering the formulated policy purposes, we observe shifting paradigms and business trends. These impacted negatively on effectiveness. For example, location interest by industrial firms throughout the 1970s was met with scepticism by the Rotterdam city council, whereas locating industrial firms would have fulfilled the previous policy purposes of creating employment and achieving stable economic development. Later on, would it not have been possible to achieve a high occupation rate for the Maasvlakte 1 area earlier on? Identically, the container boom of the 1990s seems to have occurred rather unexpectedly, whereas it fulfilled the goal of providing a cash cow.

The third evaluation criteria is related to efficiency. Would it have been possible to achieve the same effects with less investment? Based on a provisional analysis we conclude that in the years 1968–2002 the function of becoming a cash cow for the port has not been met. Considering the persistent low occupation rate of Maasvlakte 1, the expectation appears fair that an identical benefit could have been met with less costs would Maasvlakte 1 have been planned more phased, with costs occurring later on during the time period 1968–2002.

The less than impressive efficiency performance of Maasvlakte 1 is mirrored in a very modest IRR of 1.8%. Including the residual value results in a rate of return of 4.9% – a reasonable result but still below the efficiency requirement of 8% set by CPB. The high residual value is related to the booming container market producing high benefits for the port.

The ex post evaluation for Maasvlakte 1 and the ex ante evaluation for Maasvlakte 2 show important differences, in particular with respect to the exploitation result and the residual value. In the ex ante evaluation for Maasvlakte 2 the results are much lower compared to Maasvlakte 1, giving rise to questions about the extent to which Maasvlakte 2 will fulfil policy requirements.

4.6 Conclusion

Some important limitations apply to our analysis. First, whether construction costs of the Zuiderdam should be included in the total cost figure for Maasvlakte 1 is subject to debate. Second, residual value determination depends heavily on the choice of discount rate. For example, the residual value for Maasvlakte 2 is discounted over 35 years. It remains questionable to what extent the ex post and ex ante analysis can be sensibly compared. Third, we have neglected negative benefits (emissions, noise hindrance, particulate matter, quality of life).

Bearing those limitations in mind, the timing of major port investment appears to be vital for the economic success of major port infrastructure investment. Business cycles and economic trends are, prior to investment, always uncertain. Maasvlakte 1 was constructed as a location for seaport-related industrial activities. However, industrial development of the port of Rotterdam came to an end in the early 1970s and instead, Maasvlakte 1 became one of the largest container-terminal locations in the world. The boom in the throughput of containers during the last 5 years of the 35-year history made Maasvlakte 1 a profitable development in terms of ex post costs and benefits. The whimsical nature of these developments related to initial policy purposes of Maasvlakte 1 may serve as a reminder for the uncertain future legitimacy, efficiency and effectiveness of Maasvlakte 2.

References

Berveling J, Groot W, Leijsen M, Savelberg F, van der Werff E (2009) Na het knippen van het lint. Het ex post evalueren van infrastructuur. Kennisinstituut voor Mobiliteitsbeleid, Den Haag

CPB, NEI, RIVM (2001a) Welvaartseffecten van Maasvlakte 2. Kosten-batenanalyse van uitbreiding van de Rotterdamse haven door landaanwinning. CPB, Den Haag

CPB, NEI, RIVM (2001b) Welvaartseffecten van Maasvlakte 2. Aanvullende kosten-batenanalyse van uitbreiding van de Rotterdamse haven door landaanwinning. CPB, Den Haag

de Goey F (1990) Ruimte voor industrie. Rotterdam en de vestiging van industrie in de haven 1945-1975. Eburon, Delft

Dicken P, Lloyd PE (1990) Location in space. Theoretical perspectives in economic geography. Harper & Row, New York

Eijgenraam CJJ, Koopmans CC, Tang PJG, Verster ACP (2000) Evaluatie van infrastructuurprojecten. Leidraad voor kosten-batenanalyse. Sdu Uitgevers, Den Haag

Kuipers B (2003) Port strategies in the nineties in Rotterdam, Antwerp and Hamburg: Rotterdam, a loser in the container market? In: Dullaert W, Jourquin BAM, Polak JB (eds) Across the border. Building upon a quarter century of transport research in the Benelux. De Boeck, Antwerpen, pp 227–247

Kuipers B, Manshanden WJJ, Muskens AC, Renes G, Thissen MJPM, Ligthart JE (2003) De maatschappelijke betekenis van doorvoer. Een onderzoek naar de zuivere doorvoer van goederen door de Nederlandse zeehavens. TNO Inro, Delft

Ministerie van Financiën (1986) Evaluatiemethoden, een introductie. Rapport van de afdeling beleidsanalyse van het Ministerie van Financiën, 3e herziene druk. Staatsuitgeverij, Den Haag

Ministerie van Financiën (2002) Regeling prestatiegegevens en evaluatie- onderzoek rijksoverheid. Ministerie van Financiën, Den Haag

Pinder DA (1981) Community attitude as a limiting factor in port growth: the case of Rotterdam. In: Hoyle BS, Pinder DA (eds) Cityport industrialisation & regional development. Spatial analysis and planning strategies. Pergamon, Oxford, pp 181–199

van Duijn JJ (1979) De lange golf in de economie. Van Gorcum, Assen

Weigand P (1997) Maasvlakte 1. Aanleg en ontwikkeling. Gemeentelijk Havenbedrijf Rotterdam, Rotterdam

Weigand P (1999) Containeroverslag op het middendeel van de Maasvlakte. Gemeentelijk Havenbedrijf Rotterdam, Rotterdam

Chapter 5
The Productivity of Public Capital in the Netherlands: A Regional Perspective

Walter Manshanden and Martijn I. Dröes

Abstract This paper investigates on the impact of public capital on production in the Netherlands from a regional perspective. Based on a simple growth accounting exercise, the results indicate that investment in public capital contributed 17–21% to economic growth in the Netherlands between 1971 and 2000. In addition, the regression estimates suggest that a one percentage point increase in public capital accumulation increased economic growth by 0.37 percentage points, but this effect could be as high as 0.82 percentage points in the periphery of the Netherlands. We find that total factor productivity was one of the most important determinants of regional economic growth. In the period 1971–2000, the contribution of total factor productivity growth to economic growth was between 39 and 52% based on the growth accounting method. In addition, regression analysis suggests that 27 65% of the variation in economic growth could be explained by total factor productivity growth. These results suggest that public capital accumulation did contribute to regional economic growth in the Netherlands, but that other factors, such as technological change and innovation, may be more important to achieve long-term economic growth.

Keywords Production function • Public capital • Regional

5.1 Introduction

Some countries, such as Greece and large parts of Spain, lag behind relative to other European countries in terms of GDP per capita. Partly for this reason, the European Commission has created the Structural Funds. For several decades, these funds have

---

M.I. Dröes (✉)
TNO, Built Environment and Geosciences, Van Mourik Broekmanweg 6,
2628 XE Delft, The Netherlands
and
Utrecht University, Utrecht School of Economics, Janskerkhof 12,
3512 BL Utrecht, The Netherlands
e-mail: m.droes@uu.nl

W. Manshanden and W. Jonkhoff (eds.), *Infrastructure Productivity Evaluation*,
SpringerBriefs in Economics 1, DOI 10.1007/978-1-4419-8101-1_5,

been used to reduce economic and social disparities in Europe. One of the main strategies has been the accumulation of public capital through, for instance, investment in infrastructure. These efforts have spawned a long line of research on the effect of public capital on production. In particular, there have been many studies that have estimated, mainly in a production function setting, the productivity of public capital from a national or supranational perspective (for an overview, see Romp and De Haan 2007; for a meta-analysis, see Bom and Ligthart, 2008). However, these average estimates largely ignore the regional differences within countries.

In the 1990s, Krugman's New Economic Geography created renewed interest in the regional disparities in economic activity and income (e.g. see Fujita et al., 1999). In particular, due to agglomeration forces, some regions (cities) seem to attract economic activity at the expense of others. Specifically, some production factors are transferred from the periphery towards the centre of a country (region), because they are more productive in the urban agglomeration. These agglomeration forces provide at least a partial explanation why some regions are lagging behind. Instead, policymakers in Europe have mainly aimed at a more even distribution of economic activity across regions. As a result, more regionally orientated estimates of the productivity of public capital are of interest to policymakers.

The aim of this paper is to provide such estimates for the Netherlands. To this end, we constructed time series of production, public capital, private capital, and labour for four NUTS 1 regions in the Netherlands between 1970 and 2000. We use these data to provide long-term regional estimates of the productivity of public capital. We compare these estimates with the contribution of other factors of production such as total factor productivity (TFP).

Previous literature on the production function in the Netherlands has mainly focused on the effect of capital accumulation at a national level (i.e. Sturm and De Haan, 1995; Sturm et al., 1999; Daal et al., 2006). However, economic activity in the Netherlands is concentrated in the West. This region consists of the major urban agglomerations Amsterdam, Utrecht, Rotterdam, and The Hague. By contrast, the North of the Netherlands is regarded as a relatively poor periphery region. As a result, the Dutch government has mainly subsidized economic activity in the North at the expense of economic activity in the West. For instance, the Selective Investment Act (SIR Act) of 1978 formalized the Dutch government's policy to create a more even distribution of economic activity across regions. This Act imposed a tax on private investment in the West. In addition, in the 1970s the Dutch government reallocated public sector organizations (e.g. PTT, IBG) from the Hague, the political-administrative centre of the Netherlands, to the North (and South-East) of the Netherlands. As a consequence, we pay additional attention to the contribution of public capital to economic growth in the North.

The remainder of this paper is organized as follows. Section 2 discusses the data and methodology. Section 3 shows the results. Section 4 provides a conclusion and discussion.

5.2 Data and Methodology

5.2.1 The Production Function

According to the seminal work of Solow (1956), economic growth is the result of changes in the factors of production in a production function setting. In this paper, we use a simple Cobb–Douglas production function[1]:

$$Yit = AitKit^{\alpha} Git^{\beta} Lit^{\gamma}, \tag{5.1}$$

where Yit denotes production for region i and year t, Ait is total factor productivity (i.e. Hicks-neutral technology), Kit is private capital, Git is public capital, and Lit is labour. The parameters α, β, and γ reflect the output elasticities of private capital, public capital, and labour, respectively. If $\alpha + \beta + \gamma = 1$ the production function exhibits constant returns to scale but decreasing returns to production (i.e. if $0 < \alpha < 1, 0 < \beta < 1, 0 < \gamma < 1$).

This paper uses two methods to evaluate the production function. First, it is possible to assume values for the output elasticities and calculate the contribution of the (approximate percentage) growth in the factors of production in economic growth on a national level and per region. This growth accounting exercise is based on the log differences of (5.1):

$$\Delta \ln Yit = \Delta \ln Ait + \alpha \Delta \ln Kit + \beta \Delta \ln Git + \gamma \Delta \ln Lit. \tag{5.2}$$

In accordance with Maddison (1987), we assume a capital elasticity of 0.3 and, given constant returns to scale, a labour elasticity of 0.7. Since we use public and private capital in the analysis, we also assume that the elasticity of public and private capital is the same (i.e. 0.15). This assumption ensures that a difference in the productivity of public vs. private capital is not due to a difference in the elasticities of these production factors.

In this simple growth accounting exercise, the growth of total factor productivity ($\Delta \ln Ait$) can be directly calculated since Ait is the only unknown factor (i.e. Solow residual). Total factor productivity acts as a multiplier on the productivity of the factors of production. It captures those factors, such as efficiency, technology, and entrepreneurship, that are fundamental to the production process. In particular, total factor productivity growth captures the part of economic growth that cannot be explained by a simple accumulation of capital or labour. As a result, we will

[1]We ignore other specifications of the production function. In particular, we do not incorporate spillover effects (see Boarnet, 1998), capital utilization (for the Netherlands, see Daal et al. 2006), and other factors of production such as human capital (see Mankiw et al. 1992). In addition, we do not investigate whether different types of public investment have a different impact on production (for the Netherlands, see Sturm and De Haan 1995; Sturm et al. 1999). Moreover, we do not use the translog production function, the VAR approach (i.e. no lagged effects), or the cost function approach.

investigate the contribution of total factor productivity in comparison to, for instance, the contribution of public capital to economic growth.

In the growth accounting method public capital is productive by assumption. In particular, the output elasticities are exogenously imposed. Consequently, in the second approach we estimate the elasticities based on the regression model:

$$\Delta \ln Yit = \alpha\Delta \ln Kit + \beta\Delta \ln Git + \gamma\Delta \ln Lit + \varepsilon it, \tag{5.3}$$

where εit is the error term. We estimate (5.3) using panel estimation techniques. In particular, regional fixed effects are differenced out. In addition, we also show a simple time series regression per region.[2] Based on (5.3), we can statistically test whether public capital is productive and if it is more productive than, for instance, private capital. In addition, we can test whether there are constant returns to scale.

5.2.2 *Data*

The estimates in this paper are based on GDP, public capital stock, private capital stock, and labour volume for four NUTS 1 regions between 1970 and 2000: the North, the East, the South, and the West of the Netherlands.[3] GDP and capital stock are measured in constant prices of the year 2000.

The regional time series in this paper are based on the annual regional economic statistics, which is a regional (40 NUTS 3 regions) disaggregation of the National Accounts published by Statistics Netherlands.[4] As of 1970, these data are published annually. The annual regional economic statistics comprise data on gross production, value added, labour input, gross profit, subsidies, and taxes. We calculated GDP per NUTS 1 region as the sum of value added across NUTS 3 regions. In a similar way, we calculated labour in terms of the full-time equivalent of employers and employees for the 4 regions.

The capital stock is based on the Perpetual Inventory Method as described in Verbiest (1997). The national capital stock in 1970 for five types of capital is provided by Statistics Netherlands. The five categories of capital are Residential

[2]In accordance with Daal et al. (2006), we estimate the production function in first differences since the time series seem to follow a unit root process. In particular, the standard Levin–Lin panel unit root test (ADF with trend) indicated that we cannot reject the null hypothesis of unit in GDP, (private and public) capital, and labour (p-values of 0.87, 0.99, 0.31, and 0.14, respectively). We do not discuss cointegration of these time series in further detail. Evidence of such a cointegration relationship is mixed (see Daal et al., 2006).

[3]The North of the Netherlands consists of the NUTS 2 regions Groningen, Friesland, and Drenthe. The East comprises Overijssel, Gelderland, and Flevoland. The South consists of Limburg, Noord-Brabant, and Zeeland. The West of the Netherlands consist of the provinces Utrecht, Noord-Holland, and Zuid-Holland.

[4]We corrected the annual regional economic statistics, called in Dutch the "Regionaal Economische Jaarcijfers," for the revisions in the National Accounts.

(e.g. houses), Other buildings (e.g. offices, refineries), Infrastructure (public and private), Transport (e.g. trucks, aeroplanes, and ships), and Machinery (e.g. machines and software). Capital in the categories Residential, Other buildings, Transport, and Machinery is mainly private capital. Infrastructure predominately consists of public capital (e.g. dikes, highways, sewerage). Hence, the public capital time series mainly reflect infrastructure investment. The initial capital stock is disaggregated into four regions based on auxiliary data on the number of houses (Residential), value added (Other buildings, Transport, and Machinery), and population (Infrastructure). Capital stock is accumulated based on the annual regional investment (for the five categories) reported in the regional economic statistics. In addition, capital is written-off based on the average life span in years per category of capital, which is published by Statistics Netherlands (i.e. Residential: 100 years, Other buildings: 55 years, Infrastructure (public): no depreciation, Infrastructure (private): 35 years, Transport: 22.5 years, Machinery: 19 years).

5.2.3 Stylized Facts

Table 5.1 shows some descriptive statistics of GDP, public and private capital stock, and labour from a national and regional perspective. We report the level and the log differences of the variables. In addition, the differenced variables are reported for three time periods: 1971–1980, 1981–1990, and 1991–2000. Data for the year 1970 is missing due to differencing.

Table 5.1 reports several important stylized facts. First, GDP, private capital, public capital, and labour were relatively low in the North, East, and South of the Netherlands, while they were high in the core (West) of the Netherlands between 1970 and 2000. In part, this spatial pattern reflects that the regions in the periphery, including the intermediary zones East and South, were structurally lagging behind in terms of factors of production and output. Instead, part of this pattern may be the result of differences in population size across regions.

The second key stylized fact is that yearly average growth in GDP and private capital between 1971 and 2000 has been relatively low (i.e. below the national average growth) for the North and the East of the Netherlands, while this growth has been relatively high in the South and the West of the Netherlands. In addition, growth in employment has been lowest for the North. This result suggests that especially the North of the Netherlands had problems to attract private investment and to achieve economic growth between 1971 and 2000.

Third, growth in public capital in the period 1971–2000 has been highest in the periphery of the Netherlands. This spatial pattern mainly reflects the Dutch government's policy in the 1970s to reduce the output gap between the periphery, including the intermediary zones East and South, and the core of the Netherlands.

Finally, there seems to be substantial heterogeneity in the growth of GDP and the factors of production across the sub-periods 1971–1980, 1981–1990, and 1991–2000. In the 1970s, public capital accumulation was high in the North, East,

Table 5.1 GDP and the factors of production in the Netherlands, 1970–2000

	National	North	East	South	West
Yearly average	*Levels, 1970–2000*				
GDP (Euros, in millions)	255,859	29,264	42,316	56,370	127,910
Private capital (Euros, in millions)	813	89	135	188	401
Public capital (Euros, in millions)	255	30	45	66	114
Labour (full-time equivalent/1,000)	5,374	505	939	1,240	2,691
Yearly average percentage growth	*Log differences × 100%, 1971–2000*				
GDP (Euros, in millions)	2.58%	2.29%	2.32%	2.96%	2.56%
Private capital (Euros, in millions)	2.69%	2.43%	2.62%	2.91%	2.68%
Public capital (Euros, in millions)	3.07%	3.11%	3.17%	3.47%	2.83%
Labour (full-time equivalent/1,000)	0.74%	0.40%	0.79%	1.04%	0.64%
Yearly average percentage growth	*Log differences × 100%, 1971–1980*				
GDP (Euros, in millions)	2.90%	5.28%	2.51%	3.08%	2.40%
Private capital (Euros, in millions)	3.99%	4.01%	3.85%	4.31%	3.90%
Public capital (Euros, in millions)	5.00%	5.40%	5.58%	6.64%	3.83%
Labour (full-time equivalent/1,000)	0.17%	0.08%	0.48%	0.57%	–0.10%
Yearly average percentage growth	*Log differences × 100%, 1981–1990*				
GDP (Euros, in millions)	2.24%	0.04%	2.09%	3.14%	2.42%
Private capital (Euros, in millions)	1.81%	1.20%	1.74%	1.98%	1.89%
Public capital (Euros, in millions)	2.36%	2.27%	2.11%	2.54%	2.38%
Labour (full-time equivalent/1,000)	0.48%	–0.16%	0.47%	0.90%	0.41%
Yearly average percentage growth	*Log differences × 100%, 1991–2000*				
GDP (Euros, in millions)	2.59%	1.55%	2.36%	2.65%	2.85%
Private capital (Euros, in millions)	2.28%	2.06%	2.28%	2.45%	2.24%
Public capital (Euros, in millions)	1.85%	1.68%	1.84%	1.22%	2.26%
Labour (full-time equivalent/1,000)	1.56%	1.27%	1.43%	1.66%	1.62%

Source: TNO

and South of the Netherlands. Especially, the North was relatively successful in achieving economic growth. In the 1980s, average economic growth in the Netherlands was low. Especially, the North and the East of the Netherlands underperformed in terms of growth in GDP and the factors of production. Although the economic situation in the 1990s improved for the North and the East relative to the 1980s, these regions still had relatively low growth in GDP and the factors of production.

Table 5.2 reports the correlation matrix between (the growth of) production, private capital, public capital, and labour. Table 5.2 suggests that growth in GDP is positively correlated with growth in the factors of production. In addition, private capital and public capital are highly correlated. As a result, the effect of public capital vs. private capital on production, estimated in a regression setup, may be hard to distinguish from a statistical point of view. As a consequence, we will also show the joint significance tests of public capital and private capital. Finally, capital accumulation seems to be negatively related to growth in labour volume, which suggests that capital and labour may act as substitutes.

Table 5.2 Correlation matrix between the growth in GDP and the growth in the factors of production, 1971–2000

	Growth in GDP ($\Delta \ln Yit$)	Growth in private capital ($\Delta \ln Kit$)	Growth in public capital ($\Delta \ln Git$)	Growth in labour ($\Delta \ln Lit$)
Growth in GDP ($\Delta \ln Yit$)	1.000			
Growth in private capital ($\Delta \ln Kit$)	0.264***	1.000		
Growth in public capital ($\Delta \ln Git$)	0.265***	0.772***	1.000	
Growth in labour ($\Delta \ln Lit$)	0.060	–0.092	–0.272***	1.000

Notes: ***, **, * denote 1%, 5%, 10% significance, respectively.
Source: TNO

5.3 Results

5.3.1 Growth Accounting

Based on (5.3) and the averages in Table 5.1, Table 5.3 shows the percentage contribution of the factors of production to economic growth on a regional and national level.[5] Again, these contributions are calculated based on the total sample period and the three sub-periods 1971–1980, 1981–1990, and 1991–2000. These contributions add up to 100%. In essence, we quantify the patterns that were discussed in the stylized facts section in terms of economic growth.

Table 5.3 suggests that about 46% of growth cannot be explained by the growth in the factors of production in the period 1971–2000. This growth in total factor productivity, for instance due to technological change and efficiency gains, is highest in the North of the Netherlands (about 52%). This counterintuitive result reflects that the growth in labour has been relatively low in the North, while we assumed that labour is an important determinant of economic growth relative to the other factors of production. In addition, the high contribution of total factor productivity to economic growth in the North between 1971 and 2000 may mainly reflect the high total factor productivity growth in the North in the 1970s.

Private capital seems to have contributed about 15–17% to economic growth between 1971 and 2000. This contribution is (somewhat) lower than the contribution of public capital since average growth of private capital has been lower than the growth of public capital.

[5] Instead, it is possible to calculate the contributions of the factors of production on an yearly level and, subsequently, to report the yearly average contribution per factor of production. However, in some years there were outliers in these ratios. Hence, we use average growth to calculate the contributions.

Table 5.3 Contribution of the growth in the factors of production to economic growth

	National	North	East	South	West
Percentage contribution to growth	*Total sample period, 1971–2000*				
Contribution of private capital (%)	15.68	15.88	16.93	14.77	15.71
Contribution of public capital (%)	17.87	20.38	20.51	17.57	16.59
Contribution of labour (%)	19.99	12.11	23.82	24.71	17.60
Contribution of TFP (%)	46.46	51.63	38.73	42.95	50.10
Sum of the contributions (%)	100.00	100.00	100.00	100.00	100.00
Percentage contribution to growth	*Sub-period, 1971–1980*				
Contribution of private capital (%)	20.66	11.40	22.97	20.94	24.38
Contribution of public capital (%)	25.87	15.33	33.30	32.27	23.97
Contribution of labour (%)	4.05	1.04	13.31	13.03	−2.89
Contribution of TFP (%)	49.42	72.23	30.43	33.76	54.54
Sum of the contributions (%)	100.00	100.00	100.00	100.00	100.00
Percentage contribution to growth	*Sub-period, 1981–1990*				
Contribution of private capital (%)	12.12	439.08	12.45	9.47	11.71
Contribution of public capital (%)	15.79	829.88	15.11	12.13	14.74
Contribution of labour (%)	14.93	−269.42	15.61	19.99	11.82
Contribution of TFP (%)	57.16	−899.55	56.83	58.41	61.73
Sum of the contributions (%)	100.00	100.00	100.00	100.00	100.00
Percentage contribution to growth	*Sub-period, 1991–2000*				
Contribution of private capital (%)	13.18	19.95	14.47	13.85	11.82
Contribution of public capital (%)	10.71	16.18	11.68	6.92	11.93
Contribution of labour (%)	42.21	57.16	42.30	43.89	39.77
Contribution of TFP (%)	33.89	6.71	31.54	35.33	36.48
Sum of the contributions (%)	100.00	100.00	100.00	100.00	100.00

Notes: The contributions of the factors of production are calculated by dividing the yearly average percentage growth of the factor (i.e. reported in Table 5.1) by the yearly average growth in GDP. The growth in total factor productivity is economic growth minus the growth in the other factors of production (weighted by their shares in production).
Source: TNO

In accordance with previous results, public capital seems to have showed a relatively high contribution (between 18 and 21%) to economic growth in the periphery of the Netherlands. This result implies that growth in these regions may have been partly artificially induced. Nevertheless, the contribution of public capital to economic growth in the urbanized West of the Netherlands, although relatively low, was still about 17%. These estimates suggest that the impact of public capital is comparable to the impact of private capital. In addition, the regional variation in the effect of (public and private) capital based on the total sample period seems to be modest.

Finally, these contributions differ over the three sub-periods. In particular, the relatively high economic growth in the North of the Netherlands in the 1970s was mainly the result of total factor productivity growth. Nevertheless, public capital played a relatively important role in economic growth in the Netherlands (i.e. between 15 and 33%), while increases in labour volume had a relatively low impact on economic growth. The latter is related to stagflation; due to the so-called Dutch Disease (excess demand), labour became relatively expensive and was substituted by capital. Inflation, low growth, and unemployment were the result. Therefore, the contribution of labour to growth was limited. The contribution of labour was even negative for the West of the Netherlands, which seems to reflect a small decline in labour volume in this region in the 1970s. Due to measures to cut down labour cost during the 1980s, the contribution of labour to growth increased. Throughout the 1980s, the growth accounting results for the North are not credible since the near-zero growth in the North during this period amplifies the impact of the production factors to economic growth. In addition, the results in Table 5.3 indicate that total factor productivity growth was an important determinant of economic growth in the 1980s in comparison to the 1970s or the 1990s.

During the 1990s, growth was mainly the result of an increase in labour volume, especially in the North of the Netherlands. Moreover, total factor productivity growth was relatively low in the North. Besides the contribution of growth in labour, growth in private capital delivered a large contribution to economic growth in the North. However, as mentioned in Table 5.1, private capital growth and, consequently, economic growth during this period was low in the North in comparison to the rest of the Netherlands.

5.3.2 Regression Analysis

The estimates of (5.3) are presented in Table 5.4. We estimated (5.3) with the pooled dataset (column 1) and per region (columns 2–5). Since the time dimension of the dataset is relatively small, we only report the estimates for the total sample period 1971–2000. The results in Table 5.4 indicate that most of the factors of production are individually insignificant at the 5% significance level. This result may partly reflect the high multi-collinearity between public and private capital growth (i.e. see Table 5.2). The high R-squared in columns 1–5 may also be an indication of high multi-collinearity. These results suggest that the effects of the factors of production on economic growth may be hard to separate from each other. In particular, the effect of private capital does not seem to differ significantly from the effect of public capital.[6] In addition, we also did not find much evidence that the effect of public and private capital growth differs from the effect of changes in

[6] We find an F-value of 0.01 in the panel regression and F-values between 0.01 and 2.81 with respect to the regional estimates. Furthermore, we also estimated standard production functions (i.e. no difference in the effect of public and private capital). In this case, the joint effect of capital was 0.83 (national), 1.15 (North), 0.58 (East), 0.68 (South), and 0.77 (West). The effect of labour was 0.25 (national), −0.69 (North), 0.75 (East), 0.64 (South), and 0.49 (West). These coefficient estimates were significant at the 5% significance level except for the labour coefficient from a national perspective and in the North of the Netherlands.

Table 5.4 Regional estimates of the production function (with public capital)

	Regression estimates equation (5.3), 1971–2000				
	(1) Panel	(2) North	(3) East	(4) South	(5) West
Growth in private capital ($\Delta \ln Kit$)	0.407 (0.194)	0.184 (0.830)	−0.496 (0.467)	0.343 (0.532)	0.172 (0.517)
Growth in public capital ($\Delta \ln Git$)	0.372 (0.167)	0.810 (0.666)	0.824** (0.330)	0.278 (0.386)	0.599 (0.482)
Growth in labour ($\Delta \ln Lit$)	0.293 (0.359)	−0.613 (0.505)	0.965*** (0.277)	0.707* (0.403)	0.509*** (0.183)
Nr. Obs.	120	30	30	30	30
R-squared	0.431	0.351	0.716	0.601	0.731
	Tests				
Joint significance all variables	535.06	13.13	19.73	17.14	26.08
Joint significance private and public capital	16.18	15.92	11.99	5.80	19.89
Equality coefficient of private and public capital	0.01	0.18	2.81	0.01	0.18
Equality coefficient of all variables	0.03	5.28	2.66	0.91	0.19
Constant returns to scale test	0.10	1.60	2.20	1.59	2.87

Notes: ***, **, * denote 1%, 5%, 10% significance, respectively. Robust (clustered in the panel regression) standard errors in parentheses. Only the F-values of the tests are reported
Source: TNO

labour growth.[7] Given these results, it is not surprising that the constant returns to scale assumption is also not rejected.[8] Nevertheless, the test results in Table 5.4 do imply that public capital, private capital, and labour are jointly significant. In addition, the combination of public capital growth and private capital growth is also jointly significant.[9]

The panel estimates in column 1 suggest that growth in private capital is an important determinant of economic growth. A one percentage point increase in private capital growth increased economic growth by 0.41 percentage points, ceteris paribus. According to column 1, a one percentage point increase in public capital (labour) growth increased economic growth by 0.37 (0.29) percentage points, ceteris paribus. These results suggest that the contributions of public and private capital to economic growth, calculated in the growth accounting exercise, may be interpreted as relatively conservative estimates (i.e. underestimation). A further important result in column 1 is that the R-squared implies that about 43% of the variation in economic growth between 1971 and 2000 is explained by the variation in the factors of production. Hence, the largest part of economic growth, about 57%, is due to an increase in total factor productivity, which is in accordance with previous results. These results imply that the accumulation of the factors of production, such as public capital, contribute to economic growth, but they may not be as important as growth in total factor productivity.

There also seems to be a substantial heterogeneity in these estimates across regions (i.e. see column 2–5). In particular, in accordance with previous results, public capital accumulation has substantially contributed to economic growth in the North and the East of the Netherlands. Specifically, a one percentage point increase in public capital growth was associated with an increase in economic growth in the North and the East of 0.81 and 0.82 percentage points, respectively. Instead, this effect was about 0.28 percentage points for the South and 0.60 percentage points for the West of the Netherlands.

Further results indicate that growth in labour volume also had a substantial impact on economic growth in the East, South, and West of the Netherlands. In particular, the low average estimate of the impact of labour on a national level may be mainly the result of the negative association (i.e. coefficient of –0.61) between

[7] The F-value is 0.03 in the panel regression and the F-values are between 0.19 and 5.28 with regard to the regional estimates. Only in case of the estimates for the North and East of the Netherlands the equality of the coefficients on the factors of production are rejected, which may be the result of the negative impact of labour (private capital) on economic growth in the North (East).

[8] We find an F-value of 0.10 in the panel regression and F-values between 1.59 and 2.87 with respect to the regional estimates. Nevertheless, the estimates in, for instance, column 1 remain virtually unchanged if we impose constant returns to scale. Only the estimate of private capital decreases to about 0.34.

[9] With regard to the three production factors, we obtain an F-value of 535 in the panel regression and F-values between 13 and 26 with respect to the regional estimates. The joint significance test with respect to public and private capital resulted in an F-value of 16 in the panel regression and F-values between 6 and 20 with regard to the regional estimates.

economic growth and growth in labour in the North. In part, this result may be attributed to the decrease in labour in the 1980s in the North, while there was still positive economic growth in the North during this time period. The estimates in column 2–5 also suggest that private capital had a relatively large impact on economic growth in the South. We have no explanation for the negative impact of private capital accumulation on economic growth in the East of the Netherlands.

Finally, the regional estimates suggest that about 27–65% of the variation in economic growth can be explained by growth in total factor productivity. Especially in the North of the Netherlands, total factor productivity growth seemed to be important in achieving economic growth.

5.4 Conclusion and Discussion

This paper investigated the impact of public capital on production in the Netherlands between 1970 and 2000. We utilized a simple growth accounting framework and estimated a standard Cobb–Douglas production function.

The novelty of this paper is its focus on the impact of public capital on production from a regional perspective. Regional estimates of the productivity of public capital are important since the Netherlands can be divided in a relatively rich core, the West of the Netherlands, and a relatively poor periphery, the North of the Netherlands. In part, policy makers have used public capital investment to mitigate these regional differences.

We have found that growth in public capital in the period 1971–2000 has been highest in the North, East and the South of the Netherlands. Especially in the 1970s, these regions accumulated a lot of public capital, which was in accordance with the Dutch government's policy to mitigate regional disparities in economic activity (e.g. SIR act). Instead, growth in GDP and private capital has been relatively low in the North and the East of the Netherlands between 1971 and 2000. Only in the 1970s, the North of the Netherlands was relatively successful in terms of GDP growth. These stylized facts suggest that especially the North of the Netherlands had problems to attract private investment, labour, and production between 1970 and 2000.

The results in this paper indicated that growth in public capital between 1971 and 2000 contributed between 18 and 21% to economic growth in the periphery of the Netherlands, including the intermediary zones East and South, and about 17% to economic growth in the West of the Netherlands. In addition, our panel estimates suggested that a one percentage point increase in public capital growth increased economic growth by about 0.37 percentage points. This effect was even 0.81 percentage points in the North and 0.82 percentage points in the East of the Netherlands. These results imply that public capital accumulation did substantially contribute to economic growth between 1971 and 2000.

Nevertheless, both the growth accounting exercise and the regression estimates indicated that growth in total factor productivity may be the most important determinant of economic growth across regions. Based on the growth accounting, we have found that between 39 and 52% of growth in the period 1971–2000 may be attributed to total factor productivity growth. The regional production function estimates suggested that 27–65% of economic growth may have been the result of total factor productivity growth. Hence, these results suggest that factors other than public capital, such as technological change and innovation, may be more important to achieve long-term economic growth.

The results in this paper are in line with the recent policy shift of the Dutch government from a redistribution of economic activity across regions toward the increase of innovation in all regions.[10] In 1999, the Dutch government formalized its commitment to increase economic activity in the North in the Langman agreements.[11] However, it remained questionable whether, especially in a small country such as the Netherlands, the government should reallocate work towards workers, while those workers could also reallocate (travel) towards work. In addition, the reallocation of economic activity towards the periphery of the Netherlands is not without opportunity costs. These reasons may partly explain why this policy has been largely abandoned.

In 2006, the Dutch government initiated the policy to increase the comparative strengths of six regions in the Netherlands.[12] This policy is in line with the regional policy of the EU for the period 2007–2013. This EU policy is aimed at increasing the competitiveness, innovation, and entrepreneurship in these regions, but it also focuses on environment protection. Hence, this policy is in line with the Lisbon agenda. About 1.7 billion Euros of the Structural Funds of the EU are allocated towards the Netherlands and will be largely used in the national program to increase the comparative advantage of the Dutch regions. The Dutch government will also invest about 1.7 billion Euros. In the North of the Netherlands five comparative strengths have been identified by the Dutch government (LOFAR, Energy Valley, Eemsdelta, Agribusiness/life science, and water purification). As a result, we may expect more inequality in economic activity within these regions. In the allocation of the EU funds, the North of the Netherlands was not regarded as a poor region. Although the North may be interpreted as a periphery region in the Netherlands, from a European perspective the differences in economic activity within the Netherlands are minor. Again, this fact underlines that investment in the comparative strengths of all regions in the Netherlands may be more effective than a reallocation of economic activity across regions to create economic growth.

Although the creation of economic growth is widely researched, it is still largely regarded as a "black box." In particular, the experience with growth-enhancing policies in, for instance, developing countries have been unsatisfying (i.e. see Easterly, 2001). It seems clear that a simple accumulation of factors of production, such as public capital, is not sufficient to create permanent economic growth.

[10]For an overview, see Oosterhaven and van Witteloostuijn (2008).

[11]This agreement was documented in "Kompas voor het Noorden."

[12]This policy was formalized in the policy memorandum "Pieken in de Delta."

Our results are broadly in line with this idea. It seems that a combination of factors, such as the right incentives for innovation and entrepreneurship, may foster economic growth (i.e. a micro-orientated approach). Finally, it is important to note that production is not the same as welfare. A broad welfare perspective of economic growth should also take into account other determinants like climate, sustainability, and quality of life.

Acknowledgements The authors would to thank Evgueni Poliakov for useful comments.

References

Boarnet MG (1998) Spillovers and the locational effects of public infrastructure. J Reg Sci 38(3):381–400

Bom PRD, Ligthart JE (2008) How productive is public capital? A meta-analysis. CentER Discussion Paper Series, Discussion Paper No. 2008-10

Daal W, Simone FND, Yelten S (2006) "Kingdom of the Netherlands-Netherlands: selected issues 2006," section I: potential growth and total factor productivity in the Netherlands. IMF Country Report No. 06/284

Easterly W (2001) The elusive quest for growth: economist adventures and misadvantures in the tropics. The MIT Press, Cambridge

Fujita M, Krugman P, Venables J (1999) The spatial economy; cities, regions and international trade. MIT Press, Cambridge

Maddison A (1987) Growth and slowdown in advanced capitalist economies: techniques of quantitative assessment. J Econ Lit 23(2):649–698

Mankiw NG, Romer D, Weil DN (1992) A contribution to the empirics of economic growth. Q J Econ 107(2):407–437

Oosterhaven J, van Witteloostuijn A (2008) Jaarboek Overheidsfinanciën 2008. Hoofdstuk 9 regionaal beleid, Wim Drees Stichting voor Openbare Financiën

Romp W, De Haan J (2007) Public capital and economic growth: a critical survey. Perspectiven der Wirtschaftspolitik 8:6–52

Solow R (1956) A contribution to the theory of economic growth. Q J Econ 70(1):65–94

Sturm JE, De Haan J (1995) Is public expenditure really productive? New evidence for the USA and the Netherlands. Econ Model 12(1):60–72

Sturm JE, Jacobs J, Groote P (1999) Output effects of infrastructure investment in the netherlands, 1853-1913. J Macroecon 21(2):355–380

Verbiest P (1997) De kapitaalgoederenvoorraad in Nederland, M&O.007. Statistics Netherlands, Voorburg/Heerlen

Chapter 6
Indirect Effects in European Transport Project Appraisal*

Wouter Jonkhoff and Menno Rustenburg

Abstract The chapter investigates EU member states' appraisal of indirect effects of transport investment. Indirect effects can be determining factors in cost–benefit analysis. They are particularly interesting because they are caused by investment-induced changes in market imperfections and national borders. Increasing mobility and decreasing returns to infrastructure networks urge for integrated appraisal of transport initiatives. Harmonisation could lead to greater transparency and improved investment decisions. National evaluation methods, however, differ widely in their assessments of indirect effects.

Keywords Cost–benefit analysis • EU • European integration • Germany • Indirect effects • Japan • Market structure • Spatial economics • The Netherlands • The UK • The USA

6.1 Introduction

EU member states predominantly apply nationally oriented appraisal methods when evaluating infrastructure investment. However, increasing mobility within and across borders urges for supranational evaluation. Especially new EU member states can expect a certain catch-up yield to investments in infrastructure due to their lagging current infrastructure networks compared to EU-15 member states. Since infrastructure networks appear subject to decreasing returns (Fernald 1999), integrated project appraisal becomes increasingly important.

*The contribution is based on research carried out for the EU-funded project HEATCO (Harmonised European Approaches for Transport Costing and Project Assessment). Useful comments by Lóri Tavasszy and Arnaud Burgess are gratefully acknowledged.

W. Jonkhoff (✉)
TNO (Dutch Organization for Applied Scientific Research),
2600 AA, Delft, The Netherlands
e-mail: wouter.jonkhoff@tno.nl

W. Manshanden and W. Jonkhoff (eds.), *Infrastructure Productivity Evaluation*,
SpringerBriefs in Economics 1, DOI 10.1007/978-1-4419-8101-1_6,

Indeed, harmonisation of transport project appraisal could provide vast advantages from a welfare-theoretic point of view. An integrated European approach does not have the distorting effect country borders have on the size of project benefits in a number of national assessments. Furthermore, a single European approach provides a relatively transparent cost appraisal, which will allow for different CBAs to be compared. This is important, as many transport projects suffer, ex ante, from overly optimistic cost estimations, complicating optimal investment decisions and leading to overinvestment (Sten Pedersen 2005; Flyvbjerg 2005).

Indirect effects play an important role in infrastructure investment, since they represent the structural welfare effects of transport projects. Although direct effects are, obviously, central in the harmonisation discussion, indirect effects of infrastructure investment on labour, housing and product markets can amount to significant percentages of direct effects. Indirect effects can be assessed in the following ways: applying shadow prices to direct effects, correcting for the behavioural effects of investment (European Commission 2008) or separately from direct effects. Because of a lack of consistency and structure in the assessment of indirect effects, an arbitrary unsubstantiated value can easily be attributed to them. This obscures the discussion concerning assessment: does the project under consideration improve social welfare, including structural welfare?

In this chapter, we attempt to take a first step in the harmonisation of indirect effects in transport appraisal. We do this by providing a theoretical framework for indirect effects as well as by discussing current practice in EU countries. Questions to be answered include "which effects should be included in what way?" and "how to avoid double counting?". We do not aim for a proposal for quantified indicators at a European level, which would be overambitious regarding current practice. Even at a national level, valuation indicators in the area of indirect socio-economic effects are limited or simply non-existent.

The contents of this chapter are as follows. We first provide a framework for analysing indirect effects. Secondly, we discuss how and to which extent two different typical European models (SASI and CGEurope) used for the assessment of indirect effects of transport policy incorporate these effects. Furthermore, we discuss how indirect socio-economic effects are currently treated in the Netherlands, the UK, Germany, Japan and the USA. Next, we present results from a European-wide survey among policy makers. Conclusively, a comparison is made between theory and practice.

6.2 Types of Effects

Which effects of transport infrastructure can be considered indirect effects? To answer this question, it is important to distinguish types of socio-economic effects of transport projects in an unambiguous way. Otherwise, the risk of double counting is introduced: counting overlapping effects can provide overly optimistic

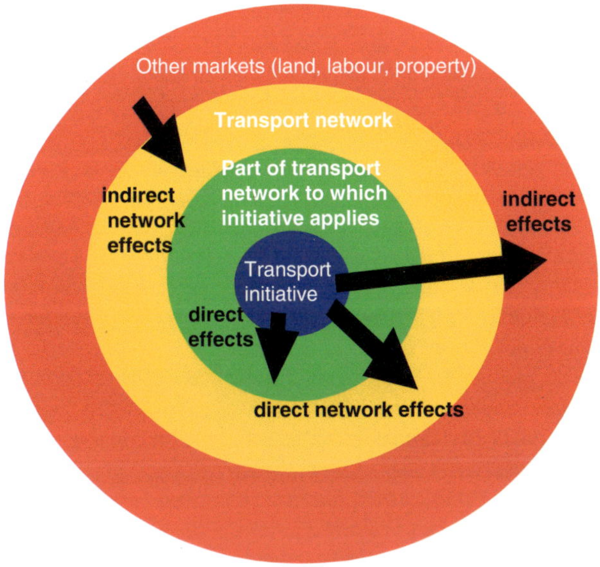

Fig. 6.1 Schematic typology of types of effects caused by transport initiatives. *Source*: Tavasszy et al. (2004)

views on projects, or the opposite, none of which is desired. Results from EU meta-research provide a useful typology to make the required distinction (Fig. 6.1) (Tavasszy et al. 2004):

Direct effects: effects on behavioural choice within the transport system (route choice, mode choice, departure time choice and destination choice), by users of that part of the network to which the initiative applies (e.g. the amount of users of a newly planned road).

Direct network effects: effects on behavioural choice within the transport system (route choice, mode choice, departure time choice and destination choice), transferred by network flows to other users of the network who are not themselves users of the part of the network to which the initiative applies (e.g. the change in train use in the area where the new road is planned).

Indirect effects: effects outside the transport market as the result of a transport initiative, typically including the changes in output, employment and residential population at particular locations implied by the choices described above (e.g. households moving to a city because it has better connections to their work due to a new road).

Indirect network effects: effects on the transport network of choices made in other markets (land and property markets, the labour market, product markets and the capital market), as a result of changes in generalised cost brought about by a transport initiative (e.g. the changed traffic flow within a city due to more households locating in the city because of a new road).

Indirect effects can concern investments in the economy; however, they are connected to disinvestments as well. Examples of the latter include earthquakes and flooding (Koike 2007; Jonkhoff 2009), which can have destructive effects on all types of infrastructure and the connected labour, housing and product markets.

Indirect effects occur due to changes in market imperfections. If no market imperfections exist, all markets connected to transport infrastructure function in a competitive way, and any indirect benefits will be transmitted via markets to consumers. In these cases, any indirect effects will not be additional to direct effects. An assessment of indirect effects could take as its starting point the absence of market imperfections and identify these imperfections from there. Indirect effects concern markets other than the transport market, usually identifying labour, housing and product markets.

As effects on income distribution, public finance, cohesion and urbanisation are mostly classified under indirect effects as well, one might distinguish indirect effects that take place in markets from those that do not concern markets but rather economic outcomes.

In the remainder of this section, however, we focus on indirect effects that take place in markets. We start by providing a rationale for the analysis of indirect effects.

The degree to which indirect effects are additional to direct effects differs widely throughout the literature. Additivity in this sense means the extent to which indirect effects add to direct effects in terms of costs and benefits. If indirect effects run contrary to direct effects, the term subadditivity is used.

Elhorst et al. (2004) conclude that direct effects are the most important in a CBA, as, in a general sense, indirect effects are rarely larger than 30% or smaller than 10% of direct effects.[1] Two prerequisites are identified for indirect effects to exist: market imperfections and cross-border effects.

The essence of *market imperfections* is that the supply-side price is unequal to the marginal societal cost or that demand price is unequal to marginal societal benefit. This may exist in product, labour and housing markets (the land market is assumed to be included in the housing market). If no market imperfections exist, the benefits within the transport market can be assumed equal to the benefits in the economy as a whole (Standing Advisory Committee on Trunk Road Appraisal SACTRA 1999, pp. 9). Pollution by traffic is a simple example of this: the supply-side price of traffic (fuel) does not incorporate exhaust emissions, but they do form part of the marginal societal cost of traffic. An environmental tax on fuel might, thus, increase societal welfare, as it internalises the cost borne by society to the user of the fuel. Other examples of market imperfections are incomplete markets, information asymmetry and hold-up problems. The indirect effects in markets with imperfections caused by transport initiatives may be positive or negative, to the degree that they render imperfections smaller or larger in markets outside the transport market.

[1] Larger effects are found for indirect effects of disinvestments caused by flooding; see Jonkhoff (2009).

Cross-border effects apply to distribution of costs and/or benefits between the country in which the transport project is carried out and other (in most cases neighbouring) countries. Cross-border effects can be more clearly addressed when a distinction is made between direct project and network effects, indirect network effects and external effects (e.g. air pollution in other countries) on the one hand, and indirect economic effects on the other. Direct project and network effects concern the effects of the use of the transport system by foreign citizens and companies. The question here is whether direct project and network effects are transmitted, via markets other than the transport market, to domestic or foreign citizens and companies (Elhorst et al. 2004, pp. 16). In France, for example, this type of effects is approached as a negative effect, as benefits of the transport projects are "leaking away" to another country, e.g. when a motorway is constructed close to the border and renders road transport in a neighbouring country faster or cheaper.

6.3 The Case for Harmonisation

To which extent are indirect effects important in the European context? Market imperfections seem to play a relatively important role in Europe. In product markets subject to international competition (*exposed* sectors), outward protection via import barriers is an important policy instrument. Agricultural markets are, perhaps, the most significant: The EU keeps world prices high by imposing considerable import barriers and guaranteeing minimum prices to its farmers, and supplying the excess supply on the world market. The internal market in the EU is free. Despite a recent trend towards lowering market disturbances and subsidies to agriculture, lack of competition from outside the EU and price manipulation can be identified as relevant imperfections. Other exposed industries feature similar protection or subsidy initiatives by governments, predominantly pointed at outward protection.

The labour market is usually heterogeneous. Relative unemployment figures for Europe indicate that supply does not match demand very well. Notable examples of market imperfections include income tax, layoff protection, minimum wages, social insurance and labour subsidies. Another rigidity is the low level of labour mobility: A majority of the workforce (except, perhaps, the highly educated) are not willing to move to another country or region for another job. With regard to the heterogeneous nature of the labour force, 4% unemployment is considered a natural rate, allowing workers ample search time for fitting employment. However, Europe features unemployment rates which are considerably higher, even during upward trends in the business cycle.

The same concerns the housing market, be it from a somewhat more theoretical point of view. The housing market is characterised by differing market imperfections. Spatial external effects include noise and visual hindrance. Spatial planning puts restrictions on the different purposes to which land can be used. Private housing is in many EU member states featured by income subsidies, while rental housing features typically public provision of rental houses and downward price regulation. However, national differences in policy and resulting market imperfections are considerable.

Harmonisation in a European context would deliver a single method for appraisal of indirect effects; these, in turn, can help to render market imperfections more transparent. The case for harmonising transport project appraisal becomes even more apparent if we look at the second source for indirect effects: borders. For example, if a road in country A is used by citizens of country B, the effect of the latter doing so is currently not taken into account. Harmonisation of method would allow for more transparency. Second, harmonisation of projects reduces the length of borders involved. Not the internal national borders will be defining but the EU borders. It goes without saying that these are far shorter than the national borders taken together. Since indirect effects in the form of travel time gains leaking away abroad do not represent loss of welfare but transfer of welfare to the neighbouring countries concerned, integral EU assessments will provide a more inclusive overview of effects across member states' borders.

Furthermore, an integral assessment of benefits enables a corresponding view to the finance of investment projects. Admittedly, a European perspective on allocation of public resources runs the risk of subsidiarity problems: European authorities are less well-informed about the necessity of local transport initiatives than lower bodies of government. Therefore, transport investment decisions should be taken at the lowest possible level of decision making. However, if we look at the current trends of increasing world trade and upward mobility, the need for transport axes with European significance seems to gain momentum. Integral assessment provides a better view to decreasing returns to transport networks and optimal spending of financial resources in the European sense. This might limit the current overinvestment in infrastructure (Flyvbjerg 2005) by putting external checks on national cost–benefit assessments and by providing an integrated allocation perspective. For example, one euro of investment in a motorway network might yield a higher return in a country starting to construct motorways compared to a country already possessing an extensive motorway network (Fernald 1999).

6.4 Current Practice

6.4.1 Models

To avoid double counting, it is crucial to distinguish the sources of genuine additionality to direct effects (Mackie et al. 2001, pp. 18). The starting point of the analysis should, therefore, be markets with perfect competition (constant returns to scale, no externalities) without borders. In this situation, no (sub)additivity of indirect effects will apply. From this starting point, one can assess market imperfections such as monopoly, monopsony, increasing returns to scale, externalities, information asymmetry, etc. It is, thus, important that market failure be reflected in models used for transport project appraisal. Models should take account of changed behaviour by economic agents after the investment. Computable General Equilibrium (CGEs) can provide these. However, they do not occur for spatial effects like agglomeration and increasing returns. Therefore, Spatial Computable General Equilibrium Models (SCGEs) are usually preferred. However, these models need large amounts of data, since they calculate on the regional level, rather than on the national level.

Now, how is this carried out in practice? For illustration, we discuss two state-of-the-art models developed within the IASON-framework, SASI and CGEurope (Table 6.1).

6.4.1.1 The SASI Model

This model, developed within the IASON-framework, is described as a quasi-production function model. The main focus of the model is on the spatial effects of major changes in transport infrastructure and pricing policy. To measure the spatial effects, Europe is divided in 1,341 regions, including the world outside Europe. Boundaries exist in the model on economic and demographic developments in Europe. Because of this, SASI delivers distributive effects, not generative effects. The model explains the regional distribution of production, which is determined by the production factors labour, capital, knowledge and regional accessibility. In the long run, all these are assumed to be flexible. Account is, thus, taken of regional migration by companies and citizens; hence, regional unemployment can be measured as well. Effects of incomplete competition can be added to change in production ex post per sector per region. No account is taken of economies of scale, neither of product differentiation (and hence monopolistic competition). On the basis of the changes in employment and labour supply the model generates, additional matching costs on the labour market can be calculated ex post. A distinction is made between levels of education. It is unclear, however, whether these are used in the production function. The model takes account of changes in participation levels, depending on the regional number of available jobs (or, opposite, on the level of unemployment) in the previous year. The fact that macro-feedback on the labour market is used enables good distributive estimations. Production redistribution incorporates foreign regions. The model does not include a land market, but the effects of change in the pressure on land due to migrating firms and citizens can be estimated ex post via relocation of production and migration of households.

All in all, this model seems appropriate to look at equity effects (the outcomes identified in Sect. 6.2) rather than large generative effects (Tavasszy et al. 2004, pp. 7). It is, however, possible to review economies of scale and relocation of production and work on an ad hoc basis.

Table 6.1 Coverage of indirect effects in SASI and CGEurope

Model	Product markets			Labour market: rigidities			Knowledge and Innovation: spillovers (external effects)	International effects		Land market: spatial policy restrictions and subsidies		Cost of tax collection
	Price ≠ marginal costs	Economies of scale	Product differentiation	Matching supply/demand	Geographical scope: Qualitative	Geographical scope: Quantitative		Direct relocation production and work	Macroeconomic feedback	Companies	Housing	
SASI	+	++	0	+	0	0	0	++	+	+	+	0
CGEurope	++	+++	+++	+	+	+	0	++	+	+	0	0

0 = not taking into account market imperfections, additional welfare effects cannot be identified from indirect effects, + = not taking into account market imperfections, additional welfare effects can be identified from indirect effects (danger of double counting!), ++ = taking into account market imperfection in a simple way (ad hoc), +++ = taking into account market imperfections in modelling in an explicit and theoretically correct manner

Source: Elhorst et al. (2004), pp. 47

6.4.1.2 The CGEurope Model

In the general equilibrium model CGEurope, the world is divided into 1,341 regions (same regional detail as SASI), connected to each other via endogenous trade relations. The model assumes monopolistic competition in six sectors with tradable goods. Interventions like product-specific taxes and subsidies can be added. The production function assumes increasing returns to scale; the degree to which these operate depends on the level of competition. Because of limited forward and backward linkages, economies of scale are transmitted, and agglomeration effects appear. The labour market is assumed to clear completely by adjustable wages. Labour mobility is assumed non-existent (this appears to be coherent to a large degree with EU practice). Like the SASI model, the model does not include a land market. Because CGEurope is a general equilibrium model, effects appear immediately and not gradually over time. According to Elhorst et al. (2004, pp. 59) the model can be used very well for all types of infrastructure. Like the SASI model, however, rigidities in the labour and land market, and hence indirect effects, do not appear to get full coverage.

These two examples illustrate that market imperfections in product markets seem to get good coverage. Cross-border effects are well developed as well. Housing and labour markets, by comparison, appear not to be completely included.

6.4.2 Current Practice in Five Countries

We now discuss shortly how transport initiatives are evaluated in five countries where transport project appraisal is considered comparatively distinct: the Netherlands, the United Kingdom, Germany, Japan and the USA.

6.4.2.1 The Netherlands

In 2000, the project OEEI project was completed.[2] It aimed at providing a standard for carrying out CBAs. This standard was called OEI-leidraad. In the following years, the OEEI standard was applied to all major infrastructure projects in the Netherlands. The goal of the project was to achieve more agreement about the methodological framework and to define instruments for determination of effects.

An evaluation of experiences with the standard was published in 2002. It revealed that concerned stakeholders were generally pleased with the standard. However, many possible improvements to the standard were identified. Identified possible improvements with regard to indirect effects included:

[2]OEEI was an acronym for Onderzoeksprogramma Economische Effecten Infrastructuur. The acronym was later changed to OEI, as the word 'economic' was erased to stress that the guidelines deal with all effects of transport projects, not just the economic ones.

- Pinpointing indirect effects in a theoretical, empirical and pragmatic sense
- Quantifying and monetising external effects
- Standardising more issues (e.g. rest value, risk valuation)
- Improvement of instruments for estimating socio-economic effects

With respect to the contribution to decision making, it was concluded that costs and benefits that cannot be monetised tend to be ignored by decision makers.

Nevertheless, most CBAs have dealt with indirect effects since OEI was implemented. The international effects of projects should get more attention in CBAs (Buck Consultants 2002, pp. 20–24). More should be known about indirect effects that are as yet difficult to model, implying the use of SCGE models: image, cluster and agglomeration economies. Empirical research into the labour and housing market would be very useful in that respect (Buck Consultants 2002, pp. 31–32).

6.4.2.2 The UK

The UK has an MCA in which the partial CBA plays an important role. CBA is compulsory for motorways (an identical framework is being set up for other transport modalities). Indirect effects are, however, not quantified. The method mentions indirect effects; assessments should point to which degree projects foster development of backward regions. Furthermore, it is qualitatively evaluated to which extent a project contributes to government policy. Likewise, external effects are only assessed in a qualitative manner. CO_2, noise and local air pollution are identified as relevant external effects. Harmonisation of evaluation criteria has contributed to transparency and has fostered the role of CBA in decision making (Dings et al. 2000, pp. 29–34; Standing Advisory Committee on Trunk Road Appraisal SACTRA 1999).

6.4.2.3 Germany

The *Bundesverkehrswegeplan* (1992) describes a partial CBA which is not compulsory but has widespread support. It is mainly used to discriminate between infrastructure projects in states and to decide whether federal funds are used or not. *The Bundesverkehrswegeplan* was modified in 2003. Issues not monetised (which have to be described qualitatively in the MCA) include damage to the environment, ecological damage, effects on urban development and certain project-specific criteria. The BVWP is meant to develop a coherent transport investment programme every 5 years.

Concerning indirect effects, particularly in job creation, some forward and backward linkages are included. Experts argue that the way in which indirect effects are included results in double counting (Dings et al. 2000, pp. 22–24).

6.4.2.4 Japan

In Japan, a two-level appraisal system of guidelines for the appraisal of CBA is used. In the first stage, certain guidelines are used to determine the benefits/cost ratio.

If this ratio is lower than 1.5 a second appraisal (which is in progress) is applied. The extra effects are grouped into three categories:

- Extension of cost–benefit items
- Regional factors as distributive weights
- MCA

Identified indirect effects include price changes in commodity markets, price changes in land markets and wage changes in labour markets; there is, however, no integral assessment of indirect socio-economic effects (Burgess et al. 2004, pp. 19–20). The types of effects mentioned are only parts of the total indirect effects picture.

6.4.2.5 The USA

In the USA, only environmental effects of transport projects are assessed as required by the National Environmental Protection Act (NEPA). This analysis is required for most transport projects. Other than that, no guidelines for assessing indirect effects exist. The exact structure of assessment differs by state. The scope is on user benefits (see American Association of State Highway and Transportation Officials 2003, pp. 1; Burgess et al. 2004, pp. 21).

6.4.3 Survey

In this section, we provide results from a survey on current appraisal practice. Twenty-six countries were surveyed with a number of questions concerning the assessment of indirect effects. The survey focused on three topics:

1. Are indirect effects included in the appraisal according to national guidelines?
2. How is double counting of effects avoided?
3. Which effects are covered, and which methods are used?

The types of indirect socio-economic effects distinguished in the survey include:

- Land use
- Economic development
- Employment (short term)
- Employment (long term)
- Cohesion national level
- Cohesion at EU level
- Urbanisation
- Network effects
- Effects on state finances
- Equity

Following the possible causes for indirect effects identified in Sect. 6.2, it appears useful to discriminate between indirect effects in markets, indirect effects as outcomes and network effects, and to note, however, that cross-border effects are not included in the survey.

Land use and employment tend to be the most relevant indirect effects distinguished from a market imperfections point of view. Economic development, cohesion (both national and on EU level), urbanisation, effects on state finances and equity are outcomes rather than indirect effects. These effects are highly relevant to CBA and should be assessed as well. From a welfare point of view, it is important to identify winners and losers and their respective welfare gains and losses, to decide whether to compensate or not.

6.4.3.1 Is Double Counting Avoided, and How?

In most countries, this issue is not explicitly mentioned, but in a few countries, a short rationale is given on how to avoid double counting:

- Include indirect effects only in the MCA (Czech Republic)
- Only a qualitative assessment is made of the indirect effects, and therefore, economic or financial results are not influenced (Latvia)
- There is no double counting because the indicators measure the compatibility with land use policy objectives or because equity issues are concerned (distribution of effects) (Switzerland)
- The impact is quantified, but not monetised. Cohesion objectives and descriptions of socio-economic effects are addressed in the formal guidelines. For example, in the UK, the cohesion objectives are assessed in the following way: conduct a review to assess whether it
  - Contributes to and is consistent with government policies
  - Has no overall contribution to government policies
  - Is inconsistent with government policies

6.4.3.2 General Coverage and Assessment Methods

Figure 6.2 provides an overview of current practice concerning the methods used for assessment of indirect effects. There are three main methods distinguished: CBA, MCA and QM (quantitative measurement). The category "Nothing" can mean either that indirect effects are not covered at all or that a qualitative assessment is used.

Figure 6.2 shows to which extent indirect effects are included in the national guidelines. For example, in Denmark, both CBA and MCA are used for assessment of indirect effects; however, they are not included in national guidelines. It is pointed out in the official recommendations that it is important to highlight that the CBA does not take all effects into account, and it is outlined how such effects could be dealt with. However, no specific recommendations are given.

The grey areas in the figure indicate the countries that are not included in the analysis; these are only included for visual reference.

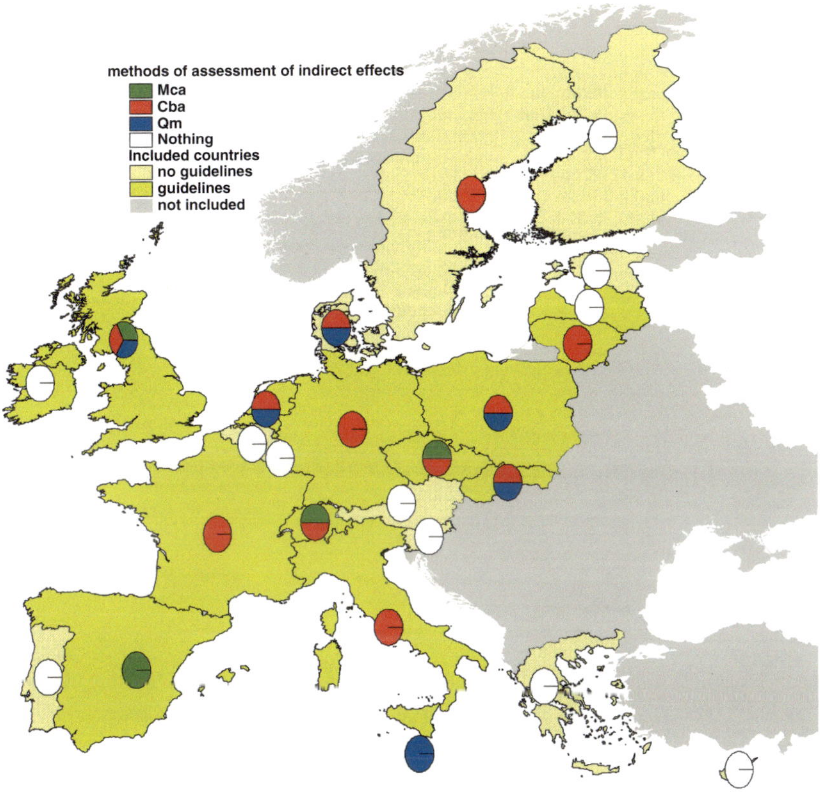

Fig. 6.2 Coverage of guidelines and methods of assessment of socio-economic effects. *Source*: TNO

6.4.3.3 Types of Indirect Effects Covered

Figure 6.3 gives an overview of the effects which are included in the assessment, regardless of the method for assessment used (MCA, CBA or QM). The most frequently included indirect effects are the effects on employment and state finances. The inclusion of cohesion effects is mainly applied in recently accessed EU member states like Hungary, the Czech Republic and Poland.

In some countries, specific effects are included (which are not listed in Fig. 6.3) like:

- Tourism, flora and fauna, landscape protection (Hungary)
- Attractiveness of cities as residence, participation possibilities of population (Switzerland)
- Improved access to seaports and airports (Germany). Valuation includes changes in transport costs and external costs, as well as impacts on regional employment. The spatial impacts covered by CBA are employment effects from the construction and operation of the transport infrastructure, and the contribution to promoting

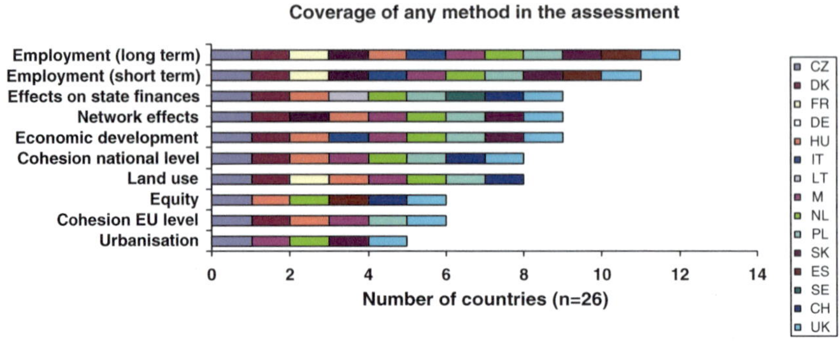

Fig. 6.3 Overview of types of indirect effects covered. *Source*: TNO

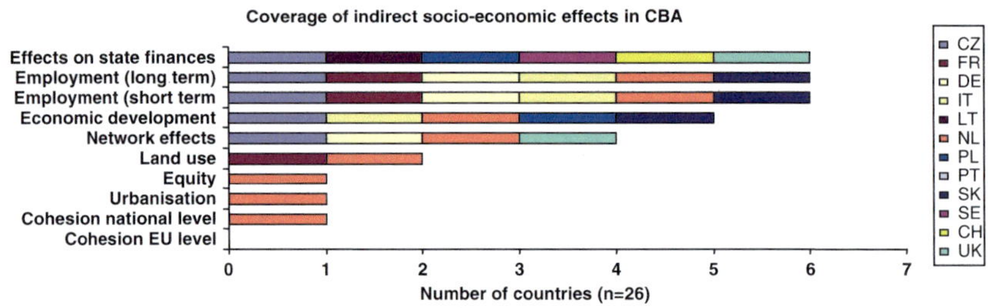

Fig. 6.4 Coverage of indirect effects using CBA. *Source*: TNO

international trade. Regional planning effects are taken into account outside the CBA within the framework of a specific spatial impact assessment

- Groundwater, animal life/habitat (Denmark, Poland)
- Project-specific issues (Latvia, the Netherlands, Denmark, Poland)

6.4.3.4 Overview of Types of Effects Covered in CBA

Figure 6.4 gives an overview of the effects which are included in CBA.

It is interesting to note that effects on state finance and on employment (in the short as well as long term) are apparently considered by and large the most relevant. Another remarkable observation from an indirect effects point of view is the low score for the housing/land market; only two countries, France and the Netherlands, take effects in this market into account in CBA. The survey shows that six countries include the labour market (the Czech Republic, France, Germany, Italy and the Netherlands). If we take a somewhat broader view and include effects on state finances, economic development, equity and cohesion (both on national and EU level), the conclusion is that 12 countries include some form of indirect effects in their appraisals. Six countries include the effects on state finances, five include economic development, and only one (the Netherlands) includes equity, urbanisation and national cohesion effects.

6.5 Conclusion

If we confront theory and practice, what kind of picture emerges? The general picture is that about half of the countries that were assessed include indirect effects of some sort in some way, but without specific guidelines on how to assess them. The analytical starting point of absent market imperfections and borders is not applied.

The gap between theory and practice turns out to be large. The theoretical and political rationales for harmonised appraisal are clear. Furthermore, sound analytical tools for assessment of indirect effects exist (be it inclusion in shadow prices, input–output multipliers or SCGE models), but they are used only infrequently and without consistency in the European perspective. Bridging the gap between the desired and the current state requires, first of all, increasingly complete inclusion of indirect effects in CBA. Second, it is important to arrive at an unambiguous standard for all EU member countries. Regarding the state of the art in current practice, it is most realistic to concentrate on the former and discuss better inclusion of indirect effects in appraisal.

For optimal assessment of indirect effects resulting from market imperfections, it appears best to combine the advantages of different models rather than using just one model. Models do not feature standardised, complete inclusion of indirect effects, so it is best to (when not constructing new models) adapt the choice of model to the type of effect (for example, urbanisation effects could need another model than labour market effects). It appears essential that behavioural changes induced by transport investment be accounted for in analytical tools and that the appropriate regional level is chosen.

The housing market seems to be the main candidate for further inclusion in modelling, since it features multiple niche markets all characterised by considerable government interventions. Furthermore, it would be a major step forward to integrate differences in education levels, labour mobility, and restrictions on labour in the form of taxes, rules, subsidies, etc. Finally, including imperfections in product markets in the EU connected to legislation on products from both inside and outside the EU markets would contribute greatly to providing a view to the performance of the EU's internal market and market policy.

References

American Association of State Highway and Transportation Officials (2003) User benefit analysis for highways manual. Washington, DC

Buck Consultants International (2002) Evaluatie OEEI-leidraad. The Hague

Burgess A, Tavasszy LA, Rustenburg M (2004) Issue analysis harmonisation; step 1: inventory of issues. TNO report, Delft

Dings JMW, Leurs BA, Bleijenberg AN (2000) Economische beoordeling van grote infrastructuurprojecten – leren van internationale ervaringen. CE/Ministry of Transport, Public Works and Water Management/Ministry of Economic Affairs, Delft/The Hague

Elhorst JP, Heyma A, Koopmans CC, Oosterhaven J (2004) Indirecte effecten infrastructuur-projecten: aanvulling leidraad OEI. Rijksuniversiteit Groningen/SEO, Amsterdam

European Commission (2008) Guide to cost benefit analysis of investment projects. DG Regio, Brussels

Fernald JG (1999) Roads to prosperity? Assessing the link between public capital and productivity. Am Econ Rev 89(3):619–638

Flyvbjerg B (2005) Uncertainty in investment on large scale infrastructure projects. Presentation held during workshop, HEATCO (Harmonised European Approaches for Transport Costing and Project Assessment), 14 April 2005

Jonkhoff W (2009) Flood assessment and policy in the Netherlands. TNO paper, OECD conference sustainable cities and climate change, OECD, Las Palmas

Koike A (2007) Spatial CGE analysis for economic damage assessment of disasters. Working paper, 53rd North American RSAI Congress

Mackie PJ, Nellthorp J, Kiel J, Schade W, Nokkala M (2001) IASON project assessment baseline. IASON (Integrated Appraisal of Spatial economic and Network effects of transport investments and policies) deliverable 1. Funded by 5th Framework RTD Programme. TNO Inro, Delft, Netherlands

Standing Advisory Committee on Trunk Road Appraisal (SACTRA) (1999) Transport and the economy. Final report. http://www.dft.gov.uk/stellent/groups/dft_econappr/documents/pdf/dft_econappr_pdf_022512.pdf

Sten Pedersen K (2005) Infrastructure costs. Presentation held during workshop, HEATCO (Harmonised European Approaches for Transport Costing and Project Assessment), 14 April 2005

Tavasszy LA, Burgess A, Renes G (2004) Final publishable report: conclusions and recommendations for the assessment of economic impacts of transport projects and policies. IASON deliverable D10. Funded by 5th framework RTD Programme. TNO Inro, Delft, Netherlands, March 2004

About the Authors

Carlijn C. Bijvoet studied economics at the University of Amsterdam and was junior researcher at SEO Economic Research in Amsterdam.

Martijn I. Droës is a PhD student in economics at the Utrecht School of Economics of Utrecht University and TNO, Delft. His specialty is house price risk and returns in the Dutch owner-occupied housing market.

Wouter Jonkhoff, a regional economist who graduated from VU University Amsterdam, is working at TNO as a researcher specializing in the regional economic impact of climate change, cost–benefit analysis and urban economics.

Prof. Carl C. Koopmans studied econometrics at Erasmus University Rotterdam. He is director research at SEO Economic Research in Amsterdam and professor in infrastructure and economics at the Free University in Amsterdam. As a head of unit Industrial Economics at SEO economic research he focuses on cost–benefit analysis and business sector research.

Bart Kuipers studied economic geography at Groningen University, where he also received his PhD on chemical industries in the Greater Rotterdam area. He is currently working at Erasmus University Rotterdam as a senior research manager port economics. He has performed research on themes like logistical development studies, port development studies, port strategy and regional transformation processes.

Prof. Jenny Ligthart holds MA, MPhil, and PhD degrees in Economics from the University of Amsterdam. She studied international and macroeconomics at the University of Amsterdam where she also received her PhD. She holds a chair in Macroeconomics at the Department of Economics of Tilburg University, an Honorary Professor of Economics at the University of Groningen, a Research Associate at CAMA (Australian National University, Canberra), Senior Research Fellow at CentER (Tilburg), and CESifo (University of Munich). Her research focuses on the macroeconomic repercussions of fiscal policy in an international context. In addition, she analyzes the economic and welfare effects of policy instruments aimed at addressing (international) tax evasion. Prior to joining Tilburg University, she worked for five years (1997–2002) at the IMF's Fiscal Affairs

W. Manshanden and W. Jonkhoff (eds.), *Infrastructure Productivity Evaluation*, SpringerBriefs in Economics 1, DOI 10.1007/978-1-4419-8101-1,

Department in Washington DC. Presently, she is a member of the IMF's panel of fiscal experts and occasionally a consultant for the Netherlands Organization for Applied Scientific Research.

Walter Manshanden studied economic geography and received his PhD at the University of Amsterdam in regional economics and works at TNO (Netherlands Institute of Applied Scientific Research) in Delft. As a regional economist he focuses on regional input output analysis, urban economics and cost–benefit analysis. He is the manager of the team "Regional Economics," working for regional, national as well as international clients.

Rosa Martin Suarez was research assistant at the University of Tilburg at the department of macroeconomics.

Menno Rustenburg received his MSc in engineering and worked as a junior researcher at TNO at Delft in mobility and logistics; thereafter, he worked as a consultant at Cap Gemini.

Made in the USA
Monee, IL
12 September 2026

62976970R00064